"Pat Ennis and Lisa Tatlock have served a rich fare of biblical teaching and practical application. With comprehensive scope and depth, this book provides tremendous motivation for obeying the biblical commands to practice hospitality—motivation that is rooted in the character and ways of God himself. Each chapter concludes with insightful questions and Bible studies, as well as practical tips and recipes. *Practicing Hospitality* will help readers grow in understanding and carrying out the biblical mandate of Christian hospitality in ways that honor the Lord."

—Bruce A. Ware, professor of Christian theology,
Southern Baptist Theological Seminary,
and Jo Diane Ware, homemaker

"When we read God's Word, there is a resounding theme when it comes to hospitality. Those who practice this ministry will not only be a blessing to others, but they too shall be blessed. This book will not only be a valuable tool for those starting out, but also for those who have already mastered the beauty of hospitality. Most assuredly, they will gain new tips and insights. Highly recommended!"

—Donna Morley, Faith & Reason Forum

"Long overdue is a careful study of the biblical teaching on hospitality. *Practicing Hospitality* will help believers recover the practice of welcoming those in need into their homes and lives, providing significant implications for the household of God."

—Mark Tatlock, vice president of student life,
The Master's College

"In a world where it's easy to focus on *my* needs and *my* wants, Pat Ennis and Lisa Tatlock draw the reader away from self and toward others. *Practicing Hospitality* inspires you to model biblical love and then equips you with practical, easy-to-apply advice."

—Glynnis Whitwer, author,
*Work@home: A Practical Guide for Women
Who Want to Work at Home*;
senior editor, *P31 Woman* magazine

"I realized quickly while in the Home Economics program that Dr. Ennis and Dr. Tatlock practice the kind of hospitality they teach. Through *Practicing Hospitality* the authors offer us a rich biblical and practical volume, and its principles will prove to be a blessing to christian women who seek to implement them."

—Robin Contreras, wife of a missionary pastor;
homemaker

PRACTICING Hospitality

PRACTICING
Hospitality

The Joy of Serving Others

Pat Ennis and Lisa Tatlock

Foreword by Dorothy Kelley Patterson

CROSSWAY BOOKS
WHEATON, ILLINOIS

Cover design and illustration: Jessica Dennis
First printing 2007
Printed in the United States of America

Library of Congress Cataloging-in-Publication Data

Ennis, Pat.
   Practicing hospitality : the joy of serving others / Pat Ennis and Lisa Tatlock.
      p. cm.
   Includes index.
   ISBN 978-1-58134-942-9 (tpb)
   1. Hospitality—Religious aspects—Christianity. I. Tatlock, Lisa. II. Title.

BV4647.H67E56 2007
241'.671—dc22

2007012234

VP	15	14	13	12	11	10	09	08	07
	9	8	7	6	5	4	3	2	1

This book is dedicated to

Hope Lian Tatlock
and
Olivia Sarah Tatlock

May you grow into women who personally understand the depth of God's love for you and his compassionate heart for the nations of the world. Because of this, may you desire to practice biblical hospitality with enthusiastic joy, dedicated hard work, empathetic kindness, and gracious character. You are both precious gifts to our family.

Contents

Illustrations

Illustrations

Acknowledgements

We are indebted to the many individuals who supported the creation of *Practicing Hospitality*. Among them we offer special gratitude to:

Dr. Tim LaHaye and *Dr. John MacArthur*—your vision to develop a character-based home economics curriculum and perpetuate it made this volume possible.

Dr. Barbara Schuch—your unselfish sharing of your editorial skills, thought-provoking comments, and belief in *Practicing Hospitality* provided momentum to keep the project in process.

Our endorsers, *Robin Contreras, Donna Morley, Mark Tatlock, Bruce and Jodi Ware,* and *Glynnis Whitwer,* who supported not only the content of *Practicing Hospitality* but also the character of the writers.

Rhonda Kelly and *Dorothy Patterson,* who reviewed the manuscript and provided helpful editorial suggestions. Special thanks to Dorothy for crafting the Foreword.

Practicing Hospitality Publication Team—your commitment to excellence made this partnership in the ministry of the written word a joy.

Acknowledgements

Dr. Mark Tatlock, my [Lisa's] husband—thank you for your consistent encouragement, dedicated love, and unshakeable belief in my giftedness. Your support allows me to participate in ministry to women in a variety of ways; for this I am sincerely grateful.

Carella DeVol—your moral support, enthusiasm, and consistent prayer on all aspects of my ministry is a constant source of blessing.

Bethany Brannon, who diligently tabulated all of the surveys used in *Practicing Hospitality*.

Jill Carter, our liaison at Crossway Books—thank you for the myriad of kindnesses you have extended to us.

Al Fisher—your enthusiasm for *Practicing Hospitality* was evident from our initial contact. Thank you for presenting our proposal to the Publication Committee, preparing the book publishing agreement, and for seeing the project through to its completion.

Lydia Brownback—what a privilege to have a published author as our editor. Your keen eye for details and editing skills have clarified the content and message of *Practicing Hospitality*.

Shannon McHenry—your careful work on the detail portion of *Practicing Hospitality* allowed us to present it to Crossway Books in a polished format.

Bailey Haigh, who carefully moved the Scripture references to the English Standard Version of the Bible.

Our students, both at Christian Heritage and The Master's College—your presence in our classes, completion of our assignments, and participation in our Hospitality Survey contributed to the compilation of this volume.

Our Heavenly Father—you established the criteria for hospitality in your Holy Word and then provided the strength to apply it to daily living. Eternity will not be long enough for us to express our love and gratitude to you!

Foreword

*P*racticing Hospitality: The Joy of Serving Others by Pat Ennis and Lisa Tatlock ought to be added to every woman's personal library. What topic should be dearer to our hearts and more on our minds than genuine hospitality! Sharing what we have with those whom God brings into our lives, however briefly, ought to be a God-inspired mandate, which becomes a heart-impelled passion. Scripture commands it; the indwelling Spirit inspires it; every woman must find ways to express it by opening her heart and home.

Hospitality has never been about having House Beautiful with perfectly coordinated accessories and the most up-to-date equipment, nor is it dependent upon having large chunks of leisure time and a big entertainment budget to spend, nor does it call for special training in culinary arts or event planning. Hospitality is about a heart for service, the creativity to stretch whatever we do have available, and the energy to give the time necessary to add a flourish to the ordinary events of life. One of the most exciting things about this book is its "anybody can" mentality, including countless ways for a woman to turn her godly intuitions into earthly service in her own humble home.

Hospitality does indeed begin at the hearth of your own home. Ennis and Tatlock are family-focused, and they make clear the biblical priority of family, including daily mealtimes, special celebrations, unique traditions, and the importance of weaving all of these into the warp and woof of your own home. Yet the authors also skillfully find ways to draw the entire family into the joy of extending hospitality beyond the family's inner circle.

The kingdom perspective is there as well. Evangelism—how better to share the gospel than to offer a cup of cold water in the name of the Savior—is underlying all. Ministries in the church and community are discussed, including ways to create cross-cultural opportunities that pull the world into your own home with a welcoming spirit evident to those who emerge from a different culture and speak another language.

Yes, genuine biblical hospitality is an art—one to be practiced and enjoyed in every season of life—and yet one that can ever be enhanced and polished. Whether married or single, with children or without, managing a household or running a corporation—a Christian woman who begins this book will want to finish it. And she will want to put it on the shelf of her own personal library, refer to its helpful hospitality tips, and use its innovative recipes, as well as find encouragement to pursue a ministry dear to the heart of our Savior—hospitality to the saints!

Dorothy Kelley Patterson

Introduction

What do you think of when you hear the word *hospitality*? Some may think of beautifully decorated homes and menus filled with gourmet foods, while others may simply think of a beloved grandmother offering tea in a china cup. The answer to the question, "What makes a person or home hospitable?" is the purpose of *Practicing Hospitality*. Throughout its pages you will be encouraged to define and practice hospitality from a biblical perspective (Rom. 12:13). The foundational principle for the book is found in Hebrews 13:2, which admonishes, "Do not neglect to show hospitality to strangers."

Our book focuses on developing both the Christian character and practical skills so that the act of *hospitality* is a joy for the host and hostess and a source of encouragement for the guest. This book is a collaborative effort. Each of us has very different life experiences related to practicing hospitality, but we share a common commitment to biblical truth. Hopefully, this will be an encouragement for you to consider how you can uniquely and creatively practice *hospitality*.

Pat wrote chapters 1, 5, 6, and 8. Chapter 1 uses the letters forming the word *hospitality* to identify key character qualities that motivate its implementation. Chapter 5 challenges believers to use their home as a center for hospitality, while chapter 6 focuses on God's special instructions to extend hospitality to others. Chapter 8 motivates believers to cultivate a heart for hospitality and provides practical tips for implementing it.

Lisa wrote chapters 2, 3, 4, and 7. Chapter 2 suggests hospitality is important for all believers to practice because it models God's love for needy people. Chapter 3 considers unique issues related to practicing hospitality with a family and emphasizes the importance of first meeting your family's needs. Chapter 4 offers practical management strategies to assist you in effectively practicing hospitality. Chapter 7 considers the implications of culture on practicing hospitality.

Our book integrates the results of a "Hospitality Survey"[1] completed by graduates from the Home Economics-Family and Consumer Sciences departments of Christian Heritage and The Master's College. Their practical advice is sprinkled throughout the book and provides meaningful examples of how to live out the principles discussed in it.

Each chapter concludes with recipe resources and projects that provide you with an opportunity to personally apply its content. It is our prayer that as you read through *Practicing Hospitality* you will be motivated to become a believer who joyfully (1 Pet. 4:9) and sincerely loves both friends and strangers through biblical hospitality (Heb.13:2).

Hospitality and Character

More than that, we rejoice in our sufferings, knowing that suffering produces endurance, and endurance produces character, and character produces hope.

—ROMANS 5:3–4

Character—what is it? "For those whom he foreknew he also predestined to be conformed to the image of his Son" (Rom. 8:29). The desire to encourage twenty-first-century society to embrace some form of ethical values is evident in the establishment of numerous secular organizations, including the Josephson Institute, at which the sole purpose is to remind the culture that "character does count."[1] Their literature suggests that a person of character:

- is a good person, someone to look up to and admire;
- knows the difference between right and wrong and always tries to do what is right;
- sets a good example for everyone;
- makes the world a better place;
- lives according to the "Six Pillars of Character": trustworthiness, respect, responsibility, fairness, caring, and citizenship.[2]

As a member of twenty-first-century society, I can certainly affirm their definition of a person of character; however, as I ponder the definition, I find myself searching for a standard by which to measure my application of it. Because I am a Christian first and a member of society second, I am blessed to have the Word of God as a standard that challenges me to cultivate a lifestyle that conforms me to the only Person who exhibited character in its purest form—Jesus Christ. Daily it is my prayer that I can say to those whose lives I touch, "Be imitators of me, as I am of Christ" (1 Cor. 11:1). As well, as I internalize my heavenly Father's Word, I am challenged to embrace his standard of *femininity*—a quality that, from a biblical perspective, has little to do with appearance and everything to do with character.[3]

Since we are blending hospitality and character, let's take a survey of the Scriptures and create a word collage of what a person of character who desires to practice hospitality might look like. Our collage could be labeled:

A Person of Christian Character Who Practices Hospitality Is . . .

H—Humble

"Clothe yourselves, all of you, with humility toward one another, for 'God opposes the proud but gives grace to the humble'" (1 Pet. 5:5). Humility is the most foundational Christian virtue and is the quality of character commanded in the first beatitude, according to Matthew 5:3. Being *poor in spirit* (humble) is to be the opposite of self-sufficient. It speaks of the deep humility of recognizing our utter spiritual bankruptcy apart from God. It describes those who are acutely conscious of their lostness and hopelessness apart from divine grace.[4] Humility, according to Micah 6:8, is a necessary prerequisite if we are going to be of service to our heavenly Father.

The evidence of my application of this quality is demonstrated when I choose to step out of my comfort zone and invite into my home individuals with whom I may not be totally at ease, or those who may have unrealistic expectations about the event because, after all, I am a professional home economist. I am comforted, however, when I look into my "spiritual closet" and find the perfect garment for this occasion, the garment of humility. When I don this garment I am reminded that I am not too good to serve—and this is pleasing to my heavenly Father (1 Pet. 5:5).

Though I entertain throughout the year, probably the most significant event that occurs at our home the last Friday of each spring semester is the Home Economics Department's senior dessert. Quite frankly, it is not a convenient time to entertain—the end-of-the-year activities, campus responsibilities, and paper grading impact my already busy schedule. Satan could easily discourage me by suggesting, as I prepare the dessert, clean the house, set up tables and chairs so that everyone can be comfortably seated, and put the devotion in order, that perhaps it is unnecessary for me to add this event to my already busy schedule. However, instead of allowing Satan's lie to take root in my heart, I choose to focus on the act of selfless service that was taught by my Lord as he washed his disciples' feet (John 13:1–17). The shift in my attitude brings to remembrance that this is one of the last opportunities I have to model to my "younger women" (Titus

21

2:4–5) the character qualities I sought to integrate into their lives during their academic sojourn.

With my Lord's model preeminent, the evening becomes one of tenderness and affirmation as we celebrate this major milestone. Later, as our home is put back into order from the evening's event, I am reminded that memories take time and energy to create—and I may have taught my "younger women" more lessons that one evening than during the entirety of their college education. As you consider performing acts of hospitality, is *humility* your foundational Christian virtue?

O—Obedient

"Behold, to obey is better than sacrifice" (1 Sam. 15:22). The words of John 14:15, 21–24 clearly identify that the primary evidence that individuals are Christians is their choice to obey their Father's commands. Writing on these passages, John MacArthur states: "Love for Christ is inseparable from obedience" and "Jesus emphasized the need for the habitual practice of obedience to His commands as evidence of the believer's love for Him and the Father."[5] Though we live in a world that promotes "have things your own way," I learned that to please my heavenly Father I need to respond to *all* of his instructions with an obedient spirit and not just pick those that appeal to me[6]—and that includes my response to what his Word teaches about hospitality. Let's examine his instructions.

Romans 12:13 says I am to practice hospitality—literally I am to "show hospitality" (Heb.13:2)—not simply offer hospitality to my friends. The subtitle for the section where this verse is found in my study Bible is "Behave like a Christian," which appears in a list of traits that characterize the Spirit-filled life.[7] The application is clear: if I want to demonstrate obedience to my heavenly Father, I will choose to practice hospitality.

First Peter 4:9 builds on the instruction to practice hospitality and reminds me that my attitude is of utmost importance—I am to practice hospitality without complaining! This verse challenges me to conduct a heart search to discern what my attitude is and whether I am approaching this opportunity to minister enthusiastically (Col. 3:23).

I am reminded in Hebrews 13:2 that my willingness to extend hospitality may have far-reaching implications. As we study the lives of Abraham and Sarah (Gen. 18:1–3), Lot (Gen. 19:1–2), Gideon (Judg. 6:11–24), and Manoah (Judg. 13:6–20), we learn that all entertained strangers who were actually special messengers from God. While my motive should never be to give so that I will receive, Luke 6:38 clearly states that the measuring cup that I use to dispense my gifts and talents will be the same one used to provide my needs. As I tabulated Cheric Land's survey for *Practicing Hospitality*, her response to the question, "How have you used your home as a center for evangelism?" provided a practical application to this truth:

> When we moved into our new house I asked the Lord to show me what he wanted me to do in this neighborhood. Well, one day the neighbor lady came and asked what I did to get my children to turn out the way they did, and I said it is only by the grace of God that my children are the way they are. She wanted help with her four-year-old. A few days later she called and said she needed to talk; she came over and was in tears, so I just shared with her and prayed for her right on the spot. I also had your first book (*Becoming a Woman Who Pleases God*) and had only read the first chapter and half of the second, but I gave it to her to read and look up the Scripture verses. It is very amazing the difference in her and the man that she is living with. All this took place on a day that I had scheduled down to the last minute and needed to get things done. Even though I got behind because of the neighbor I was still able to get everything done. Since this has happened I purchased another copy of your book.[8]

Cherie's neighbor may enter heaven because of Cherie's willingness to take the time to share her faith at an inconvenient time.

Third John 7–8 challenges me to extend hospitality to those involved in ministry for our Lord. It is exciting to know that as I share my home and resources with our Lord's servants, I become an active part of their ministry.

One of the requirements for church leadership, according to 1 Timothy 3:1–2 and Titus 1:7–8, is a willingness to allow others to observe them in their homes—the arena where their character is most graphically revealed. My friend Donna Morley describes the frequent twenty-first-century approach to this requirement:

> I remember once meeting a Christian woman who said point blank, "I would love to get to know you by talking on the telephone from time to time, but don't expect our families to get together. No offense—it's just that we don't entertain, and we like to keep to ourselves." After this woman's remark, I started to think how much this is becoming the norm in the Christian community. Why? Because we are living in a society that craves privacy and lack of involvement."[9]

As you consider this statement, what is your response? Are you willing to follow this command and allow our Lord to work his mysterious ways through the unique environment that hospitality provides or will you choose to "keep to yourself"? If you are involved in church leadership it is necessary to keep in focus that these verses are requirements, not suggestions!

Our graying population gives the hospitality requirement found in 1 Timothy 5:9–10 particular significance, since these verses suggest that only those widows who have extended hospitality, among other qualifications, can expect to be materially nurtured by the church. As you consider this requirement, may I suggest several questions:

1. Does your church have a plan for materially nurturing true widows?
2. Do you know who the true widows are?
3. Are you following the biblical instruction to assist in the material nurturing of widows?
4. Does your life exemplify the qualities outlined in 1 Timothy 5:9–10 so that you would qualify for placement on the "true widows" list?

S—Sincere

"For our boast is this, the testimony of our conscience, that we behaved in the world with simplicity and godly sincerity, not by earthly wisdom but by the grace of God, and supremely so toward you" (2 Cor. 1:12). Have you ever been invited to an event but felt that you were not *really* wanted? Perhaps the hostess was very gracious in extending the invitation, but either by her body language, tone of voice, or the conditions under which the invitation was received, you questioned its genuineness. When we extend hospitality, if we desire to please our heavenly Father, we need to endeavor to possess a spirit of sincerity. Philippians 1:10 provides us with the litmus, or perhaps we should say with the "pottery test" of sincerity. John MacArthur illuminates our understanding of this character quality as he writes:

> "Sincere" means "genuine" and may have originally meant "tested by sunlight." In the ancient world, dishonest pottery dealers filled cracks in their inferior products with wax before glazing and painting them, making worthless pots difficult to distinguish from expensive ones. The only way to avoid being defrauded was to hold the pot to the sun, making the wax-filled cracks obvious. Dealers marked their fine pottery that could withstand "sun testing" as *sine cera*—"without wax."[10]

Granted, there are times when we may need to deal with our attitude before issuing the invitation, but we need to "stay on our knees" until it can be communicated *sine cera*!

P—*Prayerful*

"Pray without ceasing" (1 Thess. 5:17). Scores of books instruct the believer about prayer, from purpose to posture. As well, multiple Scriptures encourage us to cultivate an intimate relationship with our heavenly Father through prayer (my *Exhaustive Strong's Concordance* lists a minimum of 464 verses under the topics of "pray" and "prayers"). As we consider prayer and its role in hospitality, let's take a moment to remind ourselves why we should pray.

- Prayer is commanded (Eph. 6:18; 1 Thess. 5:17).
- It is a sin not to pray (1 Sam. 12:23).
- Prayer gives glory to God (Dan. 9:16–19; John 14:13–14).
- Prayer aligns us with God's purposes (Matt. 6:9–10).
- Prayer results in answers (James 5:16; 1 John 5:15).[11]

Having identified why we should pray, let's move the theological reasons into practical application. We'll title our prayer rationale:

I PRAY BEFORE I EXTEND HOSPITALITY BECAUSE I—
- should have a sincere heart when I extend the invitation (Phil. 1:10);
- know that for the event to bring glory to my heavenly Father, I must have his strength (Phil. 4:13);
- want to have a heart that submits to my heavenly Father's instructions (Rom. 12:13b);
- need to approach any opportunity to minister with a "hearty attitude" (Col. 3:23);

- have a desire to wear "the garment of humility" to the occasion (1 Pet. 5:5);
- desire to have a gracious spirit in the midst of unforeseeable circumstances (Prov. 11:16);
- wish to glean from the wisdom of my guests (Prov. 1:5);
- seek genuinely to meet the needs of my guests (1 John 3:17);
- long for my extension of hospitality to have far-reaching implications (Heb.13:2);
- need to be excited about allowing others to catch a glimpse of my character where it is most graphically displayed—in my home—especially if I am in a position of leadership (1 Tim. 3:1–2; Titus 1:7–8);
- desire to stimulate conversations that are edifying (Rom. 15:1–2) and encouraging (1 Thess. 5:11) to my guests.

As we conclude this portion of our word collage I would like to tell you about how my dear friend and colleague, Glenda Hotton, chose to incorporate these qualities as she opened her home for a luncheon one warm summer day. Her kind invitation included a number of ladies of differing ages and interests, and when it was extended to me it was evident she wanted me to come. Her home and her heart were prepared for us; her gracious spirit allowed us to have a glimpse into her character. Though the luncheon was tasty, the recollection that is most vivid in my mind is the intentional conversation that led the group of eight ladies toward encouraging and edifying one another. The time and energy she expended in preparation for our time together yielded a precious memory for all of us.

I—Interested in Integrity

"May integrity and uprightness preserve me, for I wait for you" (Ps. 25:21). *Integrity* is defined as "uncompromising adherence to moral and ethical principles; soundness of moral character; honesty";[12] it is derived from the word *integer*, meaning "a complete entity; undivided, or whole."[13] As a believer, I cognitively know that Scripture calls me to a life of integrity; regrettably, society, and now often the Christian community, encourages me to embrace compromise over integrity. Scripture calls me to refuse to accept society's standards and to live apart from the world (Isa. 52:11; 2 Cor. 6:17; 1 Pet. 2:9). If I am going to be known as a *true* woman of integrity, I will choose to adhere to my heavenly Father's standards, regardless of what the mainstream of society is doing. Put into practical terms, I will choose to do what is right when given a choice between right and wrong—even when it is unpopular.

As I choose to display *integrity* when I extend hospitality I will seek to:

- follow the example of the Israelites' principle of separation from the world so that regardless of when guests enter my home, they observe a lifestyle that is consistent with my stated convictions (Deut. 14:2, 1 Pet. 2:9);
- use Job as a role model of integrity, regardless of the circumstances (Job 2:3, 31:6);
- study the Word of God and revere it as the ultimate authority in my life (Ps. 119:9–11);
- know Christ intimately so that his character is evident to all who enter my home (Eph. 3:14–19);
- cultivate a blameless lifestyle (Philippians 1:10 challenges me to live a life of true integrity that does not cause others to sin);[14]
- desire to lead a godly life (Titus 2:11–12) that bears fruit.

The classic booklet *My Heart, Christ's Home* challenges believers to let Christ settle down and be at home in their hearts as Lord of all. If I am going to exemplify integrity when

I extend hospitality, I will do as this tiny booklet suggests and sign over the title deed of my spiritual life for all time and eternity.[15] I then will be able to say with the psalmist, "But as for me, I shall walk in my integrity" as I practice biblical hospitality (Ps. 26:11).

T—Trustworthy

"The heart of her husband trusts in her, and he will have no lack of gain" (Prov. 31:11). When guests enter our homes they should sense an ambience of trust and confidence. When I consider the character quality of *trustworthy*, I am reminded that Elizabeth's life[16] (Luke 1:39–56) serves as the type of model I desire to follow. Let's take a look at what her life teaches us about *trustworthy* hospitality as we see how she responded to her guest, Mary, who was experiencing personal challenges:

- Mary had confidence that she would be welcome in Elizabeth's home even though Mary had no way of alerting Elizabeth of her intention to come for an extended visit (Luke 1:39–40).
- Mary chose to share freely her situation with Elizabeth, a relative and older woman. This action suggests that Mary trusted Elizabeth to believe the best rather than the worst about her (Luke 1:40).
- Elizabeth waited for Mary to explain the reason for her visit rather than immediately interrogating her (Luke 1:40b–41) or preempting the situation by telling her own good news.
- Elizabeth was a clean vessel that the Holy Spirit could use to affirm the Lord's work in Mary's life (Luke 1:41).
- Elizabeth offered extended hospitality to Mary (Luke 1:56). Since Mary arrived when Elizabeth was six months pregnant, she evidently stayed until John the

Baptist, Elizabeth's son, was born—not necessarily the most convenient time for a long-term guest!

Elizabeth's life prompts me to ask myself some probing questions about the trustworthiness of my hospitality:

- Am I eager to open my home to unplanned guests for an extended visit—even at inconvenient times?
- Am I projecting to others that my home is available as a place of refuge?
- Am I willing to maintain a confidence when shocking news is shared with me?
- Am I open to crossing intergenerational lines to extend biblical hospitality?
- Am I patient to wait for my guest to open the contents of her heart?
- Am I more concerned about what my guest wants to discuss than what I want to communicate?
- Am I a clean vessel that the Holy Spirit can use to affirm the Lord's work in the lives of others?

A—Adopted into God's Family

"For you did not receive the spirit of slavery to fall back into fear, but you have received the Spirit of adoption as sons, by whom we cry, 'Abba! Father!'" (Rom. 8:15). My parents adopted me as an infant into the Ennis family; they made a conscious choice to integrate me legally into their home and nurture me as if I were their biological child. When they entered eternity, I inherited all of their earthly possessions. When I was ten, they planned a special celebration to tell me that I was not their birth child but very special because they had chosen me. Their explanation made my later transition to salvation smooth, since salvation was described to me as being adopted into God's family. How could I not desire salvation when the first adoption was so wonderful?[17] As believers we were all adopted into God's family, and when we extend hospitality, our character ought to reflect the character of our adopted Father. Scripture tells us that as God's adopted children we are to:

- demonstrate a spirit of peace (Matt. 5:9);
- glorify our Father (Matt. 5:16);
- behave like our Father (Matt. 5:44–45, 48);
- assume a modest attitude (Matt. 6:1–4, 6:18);
- model our heavenly Father's pattern of forgiveness (Matt. 6:14–15);
- possess a childlike confidence in our Father (Matt. 6:25–34);
- petition our Father for our needs (Matt. 7:7–11);
- replicate our Father's merciful spirit (Luke 6:35–36);
- maintain a holy lifestyle (2 Cor. 6:17–18; 7:1; Phil. 2:15; 1 John 3:2–3).

When we choose, through the strength of the Holy Spirit, to behave in a way that reflects our royal heritage, our guests will observe a bit of heaven on earth in our homes.

L—Led by the Spirit

"For all who are led by the Spirit of God are sons of God" (Rom. 8:14). If I am going to practice biblical hospitality, I must be "led by the Spirit," or as Galatians 5:16 states, I must "walk by the Spirit." The doctrinal message of walking by the Spirit is found in Galatians 2:16, while the practical application is found in Galatians 5:16. "Walking by the Spirit" literally means keeping in step with the Spirit. It is a very practical form of living, not a mystical disconnection from reality. As a godly woman in progress I will display that I am walking by the Spirit when I extend hospitality by:

- bearing others' burdens through ministering to them in times of grief, remorse, sin, and troubles of all kinds (Gal. 6:2; Col. 3:12; James 5:11);
- sharing blessings that combine accompanying our praise to God with practical acts of kindness (Heb.13:6; James 1:27; 1 John 3:18);
- rejoicing with those who receive blessings and honor by occasions of celebration (Rom. 12:15; 1 Cor. 12:26);
- being willing to wear the physical and emotional bruises that can be associated with opening our hearts and homes to others. Paul's "large letters" served as a reminder of the physical "bruises" he bore because of his service to Christ (Gal. 6:11). "Physical and emotional bruises" may be acquired as I offer hospitality when
  - I experience weariness or emotional fatigue (and sometimes both) from having guests in our home—even when we have used good time-management skills;
  - I receive unwarranted criticism;
  - there is no evidence of gratitude;
  - it appears there is no fruit for my labor. It is incredibly important to remember that even if I receive the bruise, that does not mean I should not have practiced biblical hospitality—and if I allow it, the bruise will heal without a scar;

- purposing to abstain from the fleshly actions described in Galatians 5:17–22: sexual immorality, moral impurity, promiscuity, idolatry, sorcery, hatreds, strife, jealously, outbursts of anger, selfish ambitions, dissensions, factions, envy, drunkenness, carousing, and anything similar;
- controlling my thoughts, actions, clothing, and how I use my tongue (Phil. 4:8–9; Col. 3:17; 1 Pet. 3:1–4; James 3:1–12);

- choosing to cultivate the fruit of the Spirit—love, joy, peace, patience, kindness, goodness, faithfulness, gentleness, and self-control (Gal. 5:22–23).

I—Instrumental in Producing Righteousness

"Let not sin therefore reign in your mortal body, to make you obey its passions. Do not present your members to sin as instruments for unrighteousness, but present yourselves to God as those who have been brought from death to life, and your members to God as instruments for righteousness" (Rom. 6:12–13).

The human body is a complex instrument. Romans 6:12–14 reminds me that I am either using it as an instrument of righteousness or an instrument of unrighteousness. My body is "the only remaining repository where sin finds the believer vulnerable. The brain and its thinking process are part of the body and thus tempt our souls with its sinful lusts."[18] If my body is going to be an instrument of righteousness when I extend hospitality, I will choose, as 2 Corinthians 10:5 suggests, to take "every thought captive to obey Christ"—and that means that I must control what I think about! Philippians 4:6–8 challenges me to be spiritually renewed by refusing to fret or worry about anything, but rather, to humbly present my concerns to my loving heavenly Father—even when the hospitality event appears to be beyond my capabilities. I can implement this spiritual truth by:

- deliberately bringing thoughts of little or large need to Christ's control. This means that I
  - make my anxious thoughts known to my Lord (Ps. 139:23–24);
  - believe that what I ask in prayer I will receive (Matt. 21:22);
  - wait for his timing (Ps. 37:7; Isa. 40:31);

- casting my cares on our Lord rather than worrying about them. I choose to
  - roll my burden on my Lord (Ps. 55:22);
  - place my confidence in God (Ps. 56:11);
  - trust my heavenly Father instead of leaning on my understanding (Prov. 3:5–6);

- committing the details of my life to my heavenly Father so that each day is characterized by peace. This is accomplished as a result of
  - seeking and pursuing peace (Ps. 34:14);
  - allowing God's peace to rule in my heart, and being thankful (Col. 3:15);
  - making a conscious commitment to face all trials with joy (James 1:2);

- choosing to align my thinking according to the guidelines outlined in Philippians 4:8. This means that I will meditate on things that are:
  - true—those things that are found in God (2 Tim. 2:25), Christ (Eph. 4:20–21), the Holy Spirit (John 16:13), and God's Word (John 17:17);
  - noble—whatever is worthy of awe and adoration;
  - just—thinking in harmony with God's divine standard of holiness;
  - pure—that which is morally clean and undefiled;
  - lovely—focusing on whatever is kind or gracious;
  - of good report—that which is highly regarded. It refers to what is generally considered reputable in the world, such as kindness, courtesy, and respect for others;[19]

- directing my conversations so they reflect the application of Philippians 4:8. By doing this I will ensure that:

- my words are always carefully chosen (Prov. 25:21);
- when I speak, godly wisdom flows from my lips (Prov. 31:26);
- I will not verbally stumble (James 3:2).

Just as a fine musical instrument requires tuning by a skilled technician using a fixed standard, so my body must be tuned by the Master Technician according to his unchanging Word. May I be quick to submit to the adjustments of my Master Technician so that my body will always be an instrument of righteousness as I communicate love to friends and strangers alike.

T—Thankful

"Let the peace of Christ rule in your hearts, to which indeed you were called in one body. And be thankful" (Col. 3:15). Focusing on what I don't have or what I can't do is a common detriment to practicing biblical hospitality. If I choose to focus on the negative I will never extend an invitation to others—and home life will probably be pretty bleak for me too! As I review Psalms 103, 104, and 107, as well as 1 Thessalonians 5:18, I am challenged, by an act of my will, to extend thanks to my heavenly Father—regardless of whether I feel like it or not. As I thought of being thankful, in terms of hospitality, I recorded some everyday things that contribute to my developing a heart of thanksgiving:

- the new *heart* that I received when I became a Christian (Ezek. 11:19; 2 Cor. 5:17);
- the variety of *opportunities* that I have to share my life and skills with others (1 Tim. 6:18–19);
- the *strength* to accomplish the event—even when I am sure that I can't do it (Phil. 4:13);

- the *plates* as well as the other cooking and serving vessels that I have to prepare for the occasion. They don't have to be elegant, just consecrated to my Master's use (Phil. 4:19);
- the opportunities to practice *ingenuity* with the resources that I possess rather than using a lack of resources as an excuse to disobey my heavenly Father's instructions to offer hospitality (Phil. 4:11);
- my *table* and other furnishings that can be used as a tool to offer comfort and refuge to my guests (2 Cor. 1:3–4);
- my *abode*—the environment where I am to minister to others so that my heavenly Father's Word is *not* discredited (Titus 2:3-5);
- the *linens* I have to cover my table and the symbolism of purity that the linen fabric represents. May I be careful to share my excitement of being an invited guest at the marriage supper of the Lamb and thus cultivate an appetite in my guests to join me! (Rev. 15:6, 19:7–10);
- my *ingredients* and the prompting to recall the widow of Zarephath who shared what she thought was the last of her ingredients and found that her supply was multiplied supernaturally (1 Kings 17:8–15);
- my *talents*—both my financial resources (Matt. 25:14–30) and my natural abilities. I am challenged to cultivate them, and to be excited about learning new ones for my Lord's glory (Col. 3:17);
- those individuals who said *yes* to my invitations, and the reality that only eternity will reveal the impact of the time that I spend with them (Heb.13:2).

(If you note the first letter of each italicized word, you will find I used the letters of the word *hospitality* to create my "thankful list.")

A study of the life of Paul reveals that he learned to be content in whatever circumstances he found himself (Phil. 2:11). Because he modeled contentment he is qualified to provide me with a list of character qualities that includes the directive to "give thanks in all circumstances; for this is the will of God in Christ Jesus for you" (1 Thess. 5:16–22). As I consider my response to Paul's role model I must ask myself if I am a hostess whose prayer list of personal wants expands while my list of thanksgiving decreases, or if I choose to offer thanksgiving each time I have the opportunity to entertain. My response to these questions determines my character as a hostess.

Y–Yielded

"I am speaking in human terms, because of your natural limitations. For just as you once presented your members as slaves to impurity and to lawlessness leading to more lawlessness, so now present your members as slaves to righteousness leading to sanctification" (Rom. 6:19).

The upside-down, triangular-shaped traffic sign is an important one to notice since it is a clear warning that the other lane has the right of way, and refusing to yield may create unwanted challenges in our lives. Equally important is our willingness to yield to the heavenly Father's specific instructions in relation to practicing hospitality; in reality we are demonstrating our love to him by choosing to embrace these instructions with our whole heart—and that is when our joy is complete (1 John 1:4; 2 John 12). As I put the finishing touches on our word collage that pictures a person of character who desires to practice hospitality, I would like to tell you about Heather Lanker.

A talented young woman with the posture of a model and flowing chestnut hair, Heather was both my student and student assistant. Unaffected by her outward beauty, she focused on maturing into a godly woman during her college years. Though several young men demonstrated an interest in her, no special spark emerged from the relationships—in fact, I recall the day she reported to work with the statement, "I am *never* getting married!" I gently suggested that *never* was a long time, but she was quite firm in her resolve. Then one day Jason appeared, and I noticed that he increasingly found reasons to "stop by" the Home Economics Center.

Always polite, this handsome young man frequently stopped to visit with me; I still recall the day he told me he was going to ask Heather to be his wife. Each time I walk down the hallway in the Home Economics Center and view their picture in our "bridal gallery," their wedding picture brings a smile to my face—a wonderful combination of character and joy. As Heather continues to mature into a godly woman, her willingness to yield to her heavenly Father's instructions is more and more evident.

Jason completed seminary, and they served the Lord in a local church. Then another yielding opportunity occurred. Just recently she wrote:

> Jason just started the doctoral program at Talbot last week. He is going full time and really likes it. His only complaint is that he is out of practice with studying; it takes him longer to get through all his reading and writing. Also, he got a part-time job as an associate pastor at the church we were attending. It is a Southern Baptist church, and all the people tell us that we'd better get used to Food & Fellowship 'cause we're Baptists now! ☺ We really like it there, and Jason gets to work closely with the college and singles group, which he really enjoys. Well, today Jason preached in "big church," and here it is customary for the pastor and his wife to stand at the door and shake everyone's hand as they leave. So as I was shaking EVERYONE's hand I had this thought (it was a long line)—I had said I would never be a pastor's wife, and here I am smiling and shakin' hands; I never would have put myself here! Then I remembered your saying, "Never say *never* because God has a way of changing our plans." He certainly

has, and now I'm trying to remember what else I said that I would never do.[20]

Heather's life (and Jason's, too) is an example of someone who did not stall at the yield sign of her character development, and because she keeps merging, she experiences the joy of pleasing her heavenly Father. As we consider hospitality and character, may we be quick to yield to the "hospitality commands" of our heavenly Father.

A Concluding Consideration

The words of Russell Cronkhite, former executive chef of Blair House, the guesthouse of the president of the United States, offer a fitting conclusion to our chapter:

> Hospitality is a wonderful gift.
> We don't need a grand palace, or a dream home—
> few of us have those.
> To make others feel truly welcome,
> we only need an open heart and
> the greater beauty of love expressed.[21]

Only as I allow my heavenly Father to refine my character will I possess an open heart that allows genuine love to be expressed in my home. It is my prayer that you will join me in allowing our heavenly Father to complete the character refinement he has begun in you! (Phil. 1:6).

Practicing Hospitality

1. Table 1.1 offers a summary of the word collage describing a person of character who desires to practice hospitality. Study the table and then personalize it by preparing a table of your own following the example in Table 1.2.

TABLE 1.1

A Person of Christian Character Who Practices Hospitality Is . . .

H—*Humble*

Humility is the opposite of self-sufficiency and is a necessary prerequisite if I am going to be of service to my heavenly Father. I can exercise humility by choosing to step out of my comfort zone and invite individuals into my home with whom I may not be totally at ease, or those who may have unrealistic expectations about the event.

O—*Obedient*

The primary evidence that individuals are Christians is their choice to obey all of their Father's commands. I demonstrate *obedience* by obeying all of my Father's commands that focus on hospitality.

S—*Sincere*

Genuineness, as well as an absence of deceit or hypocrisy, describes *sincere* actions. I will "stay on my knees" until I can extend *sincere* invitations.

P—*Prayerful*

Prayer—that is, communicating with my heavenly Father—shows my desire for his direction about and dependence on him for the event. I resolve to pray about all aspects of the events that I plan.

I—Interested in *Integrity*

Integrity is choosing to do what is right when given a choice between right and wrong, even when it is unpopular. I will choose to adhere to my heavenly Father's standards, regardless of what the mainstream of society is doing.

T—*Trustworthy*

A *trustworthy* home provides an ambience of trust and confidence. I will study Elizabeth's life (Luke 1:39–56) as a model for my life.

A—*Adopted* into God's Family

Adoption is choosing to legally integrate an individual into one's home and nurturing that individual as one's very own child. I will choose, through the strength of the Holy Spirit, to behave in a way that reflects my royal heritage, so that my guests will observe a bit of "heaven on earth" in my home.

L—*Led* by the Spirit

Walking in the Spirit literally means keeping in step with the Holy Spirit. I will purpose to walk in the Spirit so I will not carry out the desire of my flesh (Gal. 5:16).

I—*Instrumental* in Producing Righteousness

An *instrument* of righteousness brings "every thought captive to obey Christ" (2 Cor. 10:5) and refuses to fret or worry about anything (Phil. 4:6–8). I must control what I think about and purpose to be spiritually renewed by humbly presenting my concerns to my loving heavenly Father—even when the hospitality event appears to be beyond my capabilities.

T—*Thankful*

Being *thankful* is an act of the will that generates the giving of thanks to God—regardless of the circumstances. I choose to *learn* to be content regardless of my circumstances (Phil. 2:11b).

Y—*Yielded*

We are to possess a willingness to yield to our heavenly Father's specific instructions in relation to practicing hospitality. I demonstrate my love to him by choosing to embrace his instructions with my whole heart—and that is when my joy is complete (1 John 1:4; 2 John 12).

TABLE 1.2

My Definition of Christian Character
and the Practice of Hospitality

H—*Humble*

My definition of *humble* is:
I can exercise humility by:

O—*Obedient*

My definition of *obedient* is:
I can exhibit obedience by:

S—*Sincere*

My definition of *sincere* is:
I can extend sincere invitations by:

P—*Prayerful*

My definition of prayerful is:
I can exercise being prayerful by:

I—Interested in *Integrity*

My definition of *integrity* is:
I can choose to display integrity by:

T—*Trustworthy*

My definition of *trustworthy* is:
I can model trustworthiness by:

A—*Adopted* into God's Family

My definition of *adopted* is:
I can display my understanding of spiritual adoption by:

L—*Led* by the Spirit

My definition of *led* by the Spirit is:
I can demonstrate being led by the Spirit by:

I—*Instrumental* in Producing Righteousness

My definition of *instrumental* in producing righteousness is:
I reflect that I am an instrument of righteousness by:

T—*Thankful*

My definition of *thankful* is:
I choose to be thankful by:

Y—*Yielded*

My definition of *yielded* is:
I demonstrate yieldedness by:

2. Develop a list of hospitality and character principles based on the content of this chapter (a principle is defined as "an accepted or professed rule of action or conduct"[22]).

3. Begin a Hospitality Notebook that will challenge you to integrate hospitality and character into your current lifestyle. You will find out more about personalizing your notebook when we get to chapter 5.

   • Use the ideas and recipes in *Practicing Hospitality* to create menus and time schedules that allow you to successfully put your plan into action.
   • Evaluate the Christian character you exemplify at each hospitality event you hostess using a chart like the one below. Include a section in your notebook for your Hospitality and Character Growth Chart.

Pat's Hospitality and Character Growth Chart

Hospitality Event (Include a Definition)	Character Strengths to Display	Character Flaws to Watch for (Include Goals for Correction)
Home Economics Department's Senior Dessert—a time with our graduating seniors and my faculty; one of the last opportunities I have to model to my students the character qualities I sought to integrate in their lives during their academic sojourn.	With my Lord's model preeminent, I choose to move forward with the event even though it occurs at an inconvenient time.	Satan could easily discourage me by suggesting that perhaps it is unnecessary for me to add this event to my already busy schedule! **Goal for correction:** Instead of allowing Satan's lie to take root in my heart, I choose to focus on the act of selfless service that was taught by my Lord as he washed his disciples' feet (John 13:1–17).

4. Using the letters of the word *hospitality,* develop a meditation alphabet that focuses on your specific needs.

- Place each letter on a separate card.
- Write the word that aligns with the letter along with your definition; be sure to focus on your needs.
- As you plan your hospitality activities, select one word to meditate upon daily from the time the planning begins until the event is executed.
- Record the blessings of the event on the back of the card. Review your blessings as you plan additional events.

Recipe Resources

Practice hospitality by preparing "portable" recipes that you can deliver to others—Iced Nuts, Chocolate Fondue Sauce, or Baked Caramel Corn. Place the caramel corn or nuts in a decorative tin, or the chocolate fondue sauce in a canning jar with a piece of fabric between the lid and the jar ring that was cut with pinking shears. Add a note of encouragement and drop off to a "friend or stranger" as you run errands.

Iced Nuts

1½ cups blanched whole almonds,
   pecans, walnut halves, *or* cashews
½ cup sugar
2 tablespoons margarine or butter
½ teaspoon vanilla

Line a baking sheet with foil. Butter the foil. Set aside. In a heavy 8-inch skillet combine nuts, sugar, and margarine. Cook over medium heat, carefully stirring *constantly*, 9 minutes or until sugar melts and turns a rich brown color. Remove from heat. Immediately stir in vanilla. Spread mixture onto the prepared baking sheet.

Cool completely. Break into small clusters. Store tightly covered.

Makes about 10 ounces or 2¾ cups

Chocolate Fondue Sauce

1 can (14 ounce) *sweetened* condensed milk
1 package (12 ounce) chocolate chips
½ cup milk
3¾ cups miniature marshmallows
1 teaspoon vanilla

Combine all ingredients *except* vanilla in a saucepan. Heat over medium heat, stirring constantly, until mixture is smooth and warmed through. Add vanilla. (Sauce can be made ahead, refrigerated, and reheated. It will keep indefinitely in the refrigerator. Add a little milk if sauce becomes too thick.)

Makes 4 cups

Baked Caramel Corn
(Tastes like the expensive, gourmet brand)

1 cup (2 sticks) butter
2 cups firmly packed brown sugar
½ cup light or dark corn syrup
1 teaspoon salt
½ teaspoon baking soda
1 teaspoon vanilla
24 cups *popped* popcorn

Preheat oven to 250 degrees. Prepare two shallow baking pans, with sides, by spraying with baking spray or buttering.

Sort popped corn to remove any unpopped kernels. Put in a large container. (I purchased a large plastic dish pan that I save for big mixing projects). Melt butter in a large saucepan. Stir in brown sugar, corn syrup, and salt. Bring to a boil, stirring constantly. Boil *without* stirring 5 minutes. Remove from heat. Stir in soda and vanilla (you'll get a reaction similar to one of your chemistry labs!). Gradually pour over popped corn, mixing well.

Turn into 2 large shallow baking or roasting pans. Bake at 250 degrees for 1 hour. Stir *every 15 minutes*. Trade oven rack position each time the mixture is stirred.

Remove from oven. Cool completely. Break apart and store in a tightly covered container.

Makes about 5 quarts of caramel corn

2

Hospitality and STRANGERS

Do not neglect to show hospitality to strangers, for thereby some have entertained angels unawares.

—HEBREWS 13:2

On an unusually warm October day the sky over my home is a beautiful light blue. From time to time a few white clouds float slowly past. However, as I enjoy the temperate weather in my comfortable home, the air is also filled with the distinct smell of smoke. Just a few miles away several fires are raging out of control. So far, thousands of acres of land have burned and over seventeen hundred homes have been lost in various communities around Southern California. The destruction is hard for me to comprehend—the number of people left homeless, the irreplaceable family treasures burned, and the difficult road ahead of rebuilding.

Concerned about several friends preparing to evacuate, I began making phone calls to offer our home as a refuge. As I talked with my friends, I did not hesitate to offer beds, food, and most importantly, a safe place away from the fires. I was sincere and emphatic, "Please come over, any time of the day or night; don't worry about calling, just come." My husband and I were prepared to give anything that would meet their needs. We were also prepared to have our friends stay as long as they needed to be away from their own homes.

As I hung up the phone and continued to reflect on the fires in my community, I was challenged to think about my definition of *hospitality*. There was such urgency in my heart to extend hospitality because my friends' lives and homes were at risk. Without hesitation I would gladly share all that I had with them. I would expect nothing in return. Sadly, however, apart from a crisis, I usually do not feel the same urgency or obligation to extend hospitality to the needy. And yet, if I truly embrace a biblical definition of hospitality, I will routinely extend hospitality with the same level of compulsion and duty as I did when my friends were in imminent danger. I will be faithful to "show hospitality" as Paul commands in Romans 12:13. However, my definition of hospitality when compared to Scripture is often lacking in compassion, sacrifice, and humility. What is a biblical view of hospitality? If you examine Scripture, you see that hospitality is *not* limited to meeting the needs of family or friends. Scripture defines hospitality as including all *needy* people—strangers, foreigners, widows, orphans, the poor, and the homeless. The fires in my community have reminded me that I often do *not* practice authentic biblical hospitality.

Defining Biblical Hospitality

"Contribute to the needs of the saints and seek to show hospitality" (Rom. 12:13). What exactly did Paul mean when he exhorted believers to "pursue hospitality"? To appreciate the significance of his command it is important to remind yourself of the context of this verse. Paul had just spent the first eleven chapters of Romans teaching about the amazing mercy and grace of God toward you and me as sinners. In chapter 12, Paul makes a transition and urges believers—because of God's remarkable grace and abundant mercy—to live in a way that is pleasing and acceptable to God. He says "to present your bodies as a living sacrifice, holy and pleasing to God; this is your spiritual worship" (Rom. 12:1). Some Bible translations use the word "reasonable" (Gk. *logic*) to explain the term "spiritual worship" in the latter part of this verse.[1]

Paul is saying that because of the great spiritual riches believers enjoy as a result of God's mercy, it is *logical* they should respond to God by offering their unwavering and dedicated service (Rom. 11:33–36).[2] After making this argument, Paul describes in practical terms *how* we can demonstrate a lifestyle that is "acceptable" to God (Rom. 12:2), or how we should live as Christians. Paul uses the last few chapters in Romans to exhort believers to be obedient because of their gratitude for God's work in their lives and their love for him. This is the context in which we find the command to practice hospitality.

Motivated by God's Love

Paul suggests one of the first ways we demonstrate our love for God is to *love other people*. He gives practical instruction on how to love people: "Love one another with brotherly affection. Outdo one another in showing honor" (Rom. 12:10). Paul is suggesting that because of God's remarkable grace and love for us (Romans 1–11), we should demonstrate our changed life through brotherly love for other people. In the list of instructions explaining how we should love others, we find the exhortation to practice hospitality (Rom. 12:13).

Hospitality is a practical way to love others. Therefore, a person practicing biblical hospitality should also be a loving person. This element separates biblical hospitality from social entertaining or even distinguishes between the hospitality of a believer and an unbeliever. Believers can uniquely display God's love as they extend hospitality. Entertaining focuses on having a beautiful table décor or preparing gourmet food. Biblical hospitality is a demonstration of love. Food and other elements are merely tools used to express our love for people. Our motivation for being hospitable women is a *response* to God's work in our lives. Hospitality is one way we can tangibly demonstrate our love for God.

Enthusiastically Pursue Hospitality

Because of God's great love toward you and me, we should *willingly* desire to extend love and service toward others by practicing hospitality (Rom. 12:13). Hospitality becomes a practical outworking of our faith. The Greek word translated "practicing" (*dioko*) in some Bible versions suggests the idea of "pursuing" or "striving for."[3] We are to be enthusiastic, eager, or passionate about practicing hospitality. "Practicing" then suggests we are actively looking for opportunities to show hospitality. Unfortunately, this is not always a woman's attitude towards hospitality. Life is busy and we often forget to *look* for opportunities to minister to others. When we do consider ways to offer hospitality, we often view them as an obligation costly in time and energy. We are tempted to focus on the inconveniences or hard work involved. But Scripture says if we are practicing biblical hospitality, we will joyfully look for opportunities to extend sacrificial hospitality. The attitude of joy suggests we are eager and excited.

Steve Wilkins illustrates the enthusiasm or passion we should have for practicing hospitality:

> The hound is given to the fox, and the cheetah to the gazelle, in the sense that each is utterly devoted to the chase, concentrating all of his strength and speed on a single object. Thus, when Paul says 'given to hospitality,' he does not mean 'perhaps you should be open to the possibility of being hospitable; don't refuse if you are asked.' As Paul would say, may it never be! The virtue of hospitality is far from being passive. We had better go after it, chase it down, and not stop until we have wrestled it to the ground.[4]

Viewing hospitality as a virtue identifies its pursuit as valuable and meaningful. In other words, any sacrifice we make in time, energy, or resources is worth it!

First Peter 4:9 teaches believers to "show hospitality to one another without grumbling." Grumbling means we are complaining or critical. Grumbling is very easy to do while extending hospitality; for example, the extra money spent on food, a guest who is late, or a guest who does not express gratitude can tempt us to murmur a word of complaint—before, during, or after the event. However, if we are grumbling in any way, either outwardly with our words or inwardly in our heart, we are responding in a sinful way to the command to "show hospitality to one another." Sins such as selfishness, laziness, and pride can creep into our hospitality. Sinful responses tarnish the joy in practicing hospitality.

The opposite of an attitude marked by grumbling is one that is cheerful, happy, or kind. These latter attributes paint a picture of a woman who is *joyful* about practicing hospitality as well as a willing *giver* of hospitality. Hospitality ultimately is a form of giving. Second Corinthians 9:7 says, "Each one must give as he has decided in his heart—not reluctantly or under compulsion, for God loves a cheerful giver." As a cheerful giver we offer hospitality without reluctance. We do not mind the sacrifices involved because we are willingly giving.

We do not extend hospitality out of obligation but, rather, we practice hospitality because of the joy we experience in giving. We freely and voluntarily give. Viewing hospitality as a form of giving helps eliminate expectations of receiving anything in return for the sacrifices made. Embracing the inconveniences, sacrificing our time or energy, and focusing on meeting the needs of others before our own, are all a part of our giving.

When people thank us for something we have given to them or done for them, we often say, "It was my pleasure"; this illustrates the attitude we should embrace when practicing hospitality. It is our pleasure to practice hospitality! Christian hospitality, therefore, is something we should practice willingly, joyfully, and enthusiastically. It is not limited to times of crisis, special needs, or holidays. It is to be a daily pursuit because of our love for people, which flows out of our love for God. We often extend hospitality when people have obvious needs—bringing a new baby home, enduring times of sickness, experiencing a death in the family, losing a job, or being caught in homelessness; hospitality should not be limited to the times of obvious needs. We should look for opportunities to reflect our hospitality in the midst of our ordinary, daily routine. The "hospitality survey" conducted in preparation for this book provides you with wonderful examples of how women practice hospitality apart from the crises of life. Look at a few of their responses:[5]

- Patti Morse shares, "We are military, so we move often. Within the first two weeks in a new home, I bake a batch of homemade cookies and take a plate of the cookies around to all my neighbors. With each plate, I write a note containing our name, phone number, and a Scripture verse. To minister to my husband's unit, I make every Monday special by sending in a back-to-work treat for them to enjoy with their morning cups of coffee. Each treat is accompanied by a special Scripture and word of appreciation."

- Lisa DeGiacomo states, "Hospitality isn't so much what you do for a friend or stranger as it is your attitude. Indeed, it does include your actions, but it is conducting yourself in a manner that is welcoming of others, which provides the occasion for someone else to be able to relax and be comfortable. This could be in your home or simply how you conduct yourself when you are with someone."

- Elizabeth Gilbert reminds us, "Hospitality is the act of sharing one's substance with kindness, graciousness, generosity, and genuine love (Luke 8:3). Just today in the midst of checking my son's job of cleaning out the van, a man happened by with a child on his shoulders. He explained he had just run out of gas; his car was parked by the church across the way, and he asked if he could please borrow some lawn mower gas just to get him to the nearby gas station. I had my eldest son run down to the shed and bring our lawn mower gas can with not much gas in it. We gladly gave the man what we had, and his immediate need was provided for. He brought back the gas can with more gas than it had held originally—a grateful man!"

- Amy Raper defines hospitality as "meeting the needs of others through the use of one's resources, specifically in and through the context of the home. Hospitality is love in action. I would also add that hospitality is not limited to the realm of the home. Anyone in any situation can exercise hospitality simply by meeting another person's needs (whether they be physical, emotional, or spiritual) by joyfully giving of herself and her resources. For example, a woman could show hospitality by sharing her lunch with someone who doesn't have one or offering a ride to someone without transportation. I believe when we extend ourselves to show love to another person we are exercising hospitality."

Commitment to biblical hospitality calls us to be generous and kind. The guidelines given to the wealthy in 1 Timothy 6:17–19 provide practical principles for becoming *givers of hospitality*; they include: be generous or liberal givers, be characterized as women who do "good works," make an eternal investment in the lives of people, and meet both physical and spiritual needs. Does this sound like practicing hospitality to you? Hospitality is simply practical love.

Hospitality Lovingly Meets Needs

"Whoever oppresses a poor man insults his Maker, but he who is generous to the needy honors him" (Prov. 14:31). Understanding the biblical definition of the word *hospitality* is important to appreciate further the exhortation to "pursue hospitality." The Greek word used for *hospitality* in the New Testament (*philoxenia*) meaning "love of strangers" is a compound word linking "love" (Gk. *phileo*) to "strangers or guests" (Gk. *xenos*).[6] This understanding is typically not how hospitality is defined by our modern society. Hospitality is still often viewed as entertaining family or friends. However, the New Testament believer understood that hospitality included strangers or those with needs. They lived in a very different world. They did not have modern-day travel conveniences such as hotels, restaurants, cars, and cell phones. One commentator says, "In New Testament times, travel was dangerous and inns were evil, scarce, and expensive. So early believers often opened their homes, especially to fellow believers (2 Tim. 1:16–18; 3 John 5–8; Luke 14:12–14; 1 Pet. 4:9)."[7]

Hebrews 13:1–2 states, "Let brotherly love continue. Do not neglect to show hospitality to strangers, for thereby some have entertained angels unawares." Once again, hospitality and brotherly love are tied together. Some translations say, "Do not forget to entertain strangers."[8] The word *entertain* can also be translated "to show love to," emphasizing the importance of not forgetting to be hospitable to guests.[9] Hospitality is a way we "let brotherly love continue."

Who Are These Strangers?

Strangers (especially believers) should be welcomed into our homes, just as we would welcome a sibling. My husband has three siblings and I have one. All are married and have families of their own. Each time we welcome one or all of them into our home we experience a unique bond of love. Our family bond as brothers and sisters is strong, unconditional, and permanent. We share parents, life experiences, and memories. Scripture uses this intimate relational example to illustrate how hospitality is a demonstration of our love for others. Most of us would not view strangers as we do a brother or sister, and yet in Hebrews 13:1–2 we are exhorted to treat strangers as family. Scripture gives us several examples of who might be considered "strangers":

- fellow believers (Rom. 12:3; 1 Tim. 3:2; Heb. 13:2);
- widows and orphans (1 Tim. 5:1–16);
- unbelievers (Luke 5:29; Acts 5:42);
- the poor and needy (Luke 14:12–14);
- missionaries or Christian workers (Matt. 10:9–11; Luke 10:7–16; Acts 16:15);
- foreigners, immigrants, or refugees—also called "aliens" (Gen. 18:1–22; Lev. 25:35).

How Do You Meet Needs?

There are many ways we can practice hospitality. The *method* of hospitality varies according to the *need* of the individual.

For example, if individuals are hungry, we can feed them. If they are in need of lodging, we can offer them a place to sleep for the night. If someone is in need of encouragement, we can listen, counsel her using God's Word, and pray with her. Scripture illustrates that there are many ways we can practice hospitality. The important point to emphasize, however, is that our focus should be to meet the needs of others. Examples from Scripture of hospitality being used to meet individuals' needs include:

- preparing food (Gen. 24:15–21; 1 Kings 17:9–16; Matt. 14:15–21; Acts 2:46; 20:11);
- providing housing/lodging (2 Kings 4:8–17);
- giving physical protection or safety (Josh. 2:1–15);
- sharing material possessions (Acts 2:44; Rom. 12:13–20; James 2:15–16; 1 John 3:17);
- offering a place to rest (Gen. 18:1–22; Mark 14:3–8; Luke 7:36–47; John 12:1–8);
- extending love and encouragement (Rom. 12:10–13; 1 Thess. 4:9–10);
- sharing the gospel (Acts 10:24; 20:20; 3 John 7–8);
- spiritual teaching or encouragement (Rom. 16:5; Col. 4:15).

We can practice all of the methods we see here in Scripture in our homes today. Regardless of the means used, Christian women who are hospitable will demonstrate love for strangers, friends, and family by meeting a guest's specific needs, whatever those may be. This pattern is the key to practicing biblical hospitality.

Hospitality Reveals Character

Hospitality is a gauge of Christian character for both men and women. It is a measurement of one's love for others.

Viewing hospitality in light of service towards others makes clear why "hospitable" was included in the list of qualifications for church leaders or shepherds. *Hospitable* is listed among the various character attributes required for church leadership (Titus 1:7–8 and 1 Tim. 3:1–2). Practicing hospitality is evidence of the character of a church leader. Alexander Strauch explains:

> The biblical shepherd is a shepherd of people—God's precious, blood-bought people. And like Christ, the Chief Shepherd, the church shepherd must give himself lovingly and sacrificially for the care of God's people (1 Thess. 2:8). This cannot be done from a distance, with a smile and a handshake on Sunday morning or through a superficial visit. Giving oneself to the care of God's people means sharing one's life and home with others. An open home is a sign of an open heart and a loving, sacrificial, serving spirit.[10]

Hospitality models God's love, mercy, and compassion toward needy people. Scripture is very clear that a Christian who shows mercy on those in need honors God himself (Prov. 14:31; 17:5). In contrast to this, Scripture questions how the love of God can be in our heart if we do not share with others when we see they have needs. First John 3:17–18 says, "But if anyone has the world's goods and sees his brother in need, yet closes his heart against him, how does God's love abide in him? Little children, let us not love in word or talk but in deed and in truth."

Hospitality illustrates the two basic priorities for all believers—to love God and to love others (Rom. 12:1–13). Jesus summarized for the New Testament believers the whole law as loving God and loving others (Deut. 6:4–5; Mark 12:29–31). The Jews of the New Testament were following the Law of the Old Testament—until Christ came and released them from the law, allowing them to live under God's grace. Matthew 22:37–40 says, "He said to him, 'You shall love the Lord your God with all your heart and with all your soul and with all your mind. This is the great and first commandment. And a second is like it: You shall love your neighbor as yourself.'" Hospitality is one of the best ways believers can "love your neighbor as yourself."

While New Testament believers were freed from the law through Christ, their knowledge of the law allowed them to have a unique understanding of God's heart for the needy. The law gave specific guidelines as to how people with needs should be treated (widows, poor, orphans, foreigners). In other words, hospitality was clearly a part of God's law. When Christ said that the whole law can be summarized by loving God and loving your neighbor as yourself, New Testament believers would have had a much different understanding of how to apply that through hospitality. We can learn much about how to practice hospitality by taking the time to briefly look through the Old Testament to see more clearly God's heart for caring for the poor and other needy people.

Hospitality and the Old Testament

"Whoever is generous to the poor lends to the LORD, and he will repay him for his deed" (Prov. 19:17). The Old Testament law was filled with rules or guidelines regarding how to live and how to treat other people (Deut. 4:1–20; Ps. 119:1). It was a system of justice for the weak and defenseless (Lev. 19:9–37). It protected those in need and promoted a spirit of generosity and giving for those who had material resources (Lev. 19:22). *Hospitality*, therefore, was an integral part of fulfilling the law.

Hospitality in the Old Testament was very different from what we practice today, and from it we find an illustration of the dedication and compassion that the early New Testament believers would have demonstrated in meeting the needs of others. The same hospitality principles found in the Old

Testament are clearly reflected in the New Testament (Matt. 25:35, 26:11, Matt. 19:21; Gal. 2:10; James 1:27).

While space does not permit an exhaustive look at every Scripture example in the Old Testament, our understanding of biblical hospitality will be greatly lacking if we do not take a few moments to look at hospitality from an Old Testament perspective. We can summarize Old Testament hospitality by saying it was viewed as a sacred duty, offered sincerely, inclusive of all people, and mutually respected.

First, hospitality was viewed as a *duty*—considered a responsibility or obligation. It was both a cultural and religious duty. Fred Wight explains this view by saying, "Guests were viewed as sent by God" and "hospitality therefore became a sacred duty."[11] Hospitality was not necessarily based on knowing the other person. People did not need to have a relationship with the individual they were inviting into their home. One commentator explains this commitment to hospitality:

> It was and is felt to be a sacred duty to receive, feed, lodge, and protect any traveler who might stop at the door. The stranger was treated as a guest and men who had thus eaten together were bound by the strongest ties of friendship, which descended to their heirs, confirmed by mutual presents.[12]

In other words, according to the custom of the day, people would sit at the door of a perfect stranger until the master of the home welcomed them in for the evening meal! An example of this custom is found in Job's words, "The sojourner has not lodged in the street; I have opened my doors to the traveler" (Job 31:32). Additional examples in Scripture are found in Genesis 18:1–18, 19:1–3, 24:25, and 31–33.

Second, hospitality was offered *sincerely*, earnestly extended from the heart. While hospitality was a duty or an obligation, it was also offered with genuine friendship. An excellent example is Abraham's inviting the travelers into his home in Genesis 18:2. He hurried to meet them and then bowed low to the ground or down on the ground. James Freeman explains this form of bowing:

> In this the person falls upon the knees, and then gradually inclines the body until the head touches the ground. See also Genesis 22:7, 12. . . . There is in this text a beautiful illustration of Oriental hospitality. The company of the travelers is solicited as a personal favor to the host, and all the resources of the establishment are used for their entertainment. See Genesis 29:2–3; Judges 6:18; 12:15; Job 31:32.[13]

Hospitality was a solemn obligation that was offered with sincerity. Nothing was withheld from the guest. The host offered complete and unreserved shelter and protection.

Third, hospitality was *inclusive* of all people. Guests fell into three categories: friends, strangers, and enemies. Friends were always welcomed guests. Extending hospitality to friends is understandable and is practiced in our culture. Hospitality also included strangers. The example of Abraham illustrates this priority, along with the verses found in the Scripture chart at the end of the chapter (see Table 2.1). An Oriental proverb says, "Every stranger is an invited guest."[14] This posture was taken towards strangers in the Old Testament. In addition to friends and strangers, Old Testament hospitality sometimes included enemies as guests. This last category is unfamiliar to us, and it is difficult to imagine one would be able to practice it; however, enemies were sometimes given food and shelter. Wight explains:

> One remarkable feature of Oriental hospitality is that sometimes an enemy is received as a guest, and as long as he remains in that relationship, he is perfectly safe and is treated as a friend.[15]

Fourth, hospitality was mutually *respected*, meaning that guests reciprocated the hospitality with a permanent and loyal friendship. Hospitality was not to be abused. Once someone had been the recipient of hospitality in biblical times, he was duty-bound or compelled never to extend evil of any kind to his host. This obligation was so binding that it passed from one generation to the next. Freeman explains:

> It is considered an act of great baseness among Eastern nations for any one to do an evil deed against those who have shared his hospitality. This feeling is very ancient, and is often alluded to by ancient authors. The Saviour refers to it when he mentions the baseness of Judas, and cites John 12:18. See also Obadiah 7.[16]

New Testament believers would have been influenced by these Old Testament principles when practicing hospitality. When Paul commanded the believers to pursue hospitality in Romans 12:13, believers would have understood it as a sacred duty, to be offered sincerely, inclusive of all people, and as a calling for mutual respect. Do you and I view hospitality with the same kind of commitment? This definition often exposes our limited understanding of hospitality.

Briefly looking at hospitality in the Old Testament allows us to see God's heart of compassion for the needs of strangers, widows, orphans, foreigners, and the poor. There is a table (but not a comprehensive list) at the end of this chapter illustrating several more examples of commands given by God to care for the needy. After reviewing the table, ask yourself what conclusions you can draw regarding your own efforts at hospitality and meeting the needs of others. Does your heart reflect God's heart for meeting the needs of others?

This discussion of hospitality began by considering Paul's plea in Romans 12:13 to "show hospitality." We were reminded to view hospitality as an obligation because of God's amazing grace in our lives and encouraged to extend hospitality with a sincere heart out of love for others. The principles for practicing hospitality are consistently woven throughout the Old *and* New Testaments because they are a reflection of God's compassionate heart. Be reminded of Proverbs 19:17:

"Whoever is generous to the poor lends to the LORD, and he will repay him for his deed."

Hospitality Defined

Now that we have briefly looked at how Scripture defines hospitality, has your understanding of hospitality changed? A look at the definitions of hospitality written by the women who participated in the survey reveals the principles examined. After reading the thoughts below, personalize the ideas by writing your own definition of hospitality and begin practicing the principles reflected.

Hospitality Is . . .

- "A love of strangers, a willingness and a desire to meet any need of those whom the Lord brings into our lives."—Melitsa Barnes
- "Opening up and sharing our lives with other people. We tend to think of hospitality as planning and executing an event, say, a dinner party, or maybe inviting someone to a restaurant and picking up the check. While these activities fall within the realm of hospitality, they cannot define it."—Bonnie Bishop
- "Being helpful and generous to others. It extends beyond the confines of the home."—Lynn Cathy.
- "Literally 'the love of strangers'—a welcoming spirit to open your home and share what the Lord has given you with anyone he brings your way: friends, family, neighbors, or someone you just met."—Lisa-Ann Chun
- "Meeting the emotional, physical, and spiritual needs of our guests in an atmosphere of warmth and love."—Sue Edwards
- "A readiness to share one's life with another."—Vicki Ferretti

- "Opening your heart and home, and freely giving all that you have to generously and lovingly meet the needs of others. Hospitality promotes and welcomes others into a warm, inviting, friendly environment where they feel loved and accepted."—Kelli Gleeson
- "An attitude of the heart, one that genuinely loves others . . . a sense of welcome when you walk through a front door, a sense of acceptance in a comfortable environment."—Anne Goad
- "A love of strangers as well as a willingness to practically meet the needs of those that God places in your life."—Erin Hair
- "Using one's resources (home, food, ideas, money) and abilities (as a hostess, cook, Christian) to minister to others in the context of your home."—Anne Johnson
- "Opening the home that the Lord has given you and sharing your gifts and talents."—Cherie Land
- "Making friends or strangers feel welcome and important when they are in your presence."—Heather Lanker
- "Defined by servanthood, striving to do for others, causing them to feel welcomed, wanted and worthwhile. The greatest setting for this is in my home, secondarily in my church, and thirdly in my employment. The ultimate goal of Christian hospitality is furthering the kingdom; in other words, will my behaviors encourage others to know Christ? Will more people be in heaven because God worked through me?"—Debby Lennick
- "The willingness to give cheerfully of your heart, home, time, energy, and talents; to extend kindness and welcome to others."—Erin McLeod
- "Showing love to strangers; welcoming people into a dwelling place with love and grace for the purpose of demonstrating Christ's love to them."—Connie Naresh

- "Welcoming people, into my home specifically but not confined to that. I can show hospitality anywhere. It's more a state of mind expressed through a variety of actions and attitudes."—Peggy Rowan
- "While entertaining is having guests with everything prepared and served correctly, hospitality is having people feel comfortable in my home and happy to be there no matter what we are doing or eating."—Laurie Twibell
- "Opening up our home to strangers as well as friends and family. I would also define it as being giving of the resources (time, money, vehicles, etc.) that God has blessed me with to reach out to others and minister to them. It is being generous and kind to others without expecting anything in return."—Maria VanderJagt
- "Entertaining others graciously without grudging or without thought of the favor returned to you."—Deborah Zacharoff

A biblical definition will reflect God's compassionate heart for meeting the needs of others. Its focus is not on the size or décor of our homes, our food preparation skills, or our home management skills.

A Concluding Consideration

Demonstrating hospitality is one practical method for demonstrating our love for both God and others (Rom. 12:13). "Whoever oppresses a poor man insults his Maker, but he who is generous to the needy honors him" (Prov. 14:31). We are to embrace the command to practice hospitality cheerfully and without complaint (1 Pet. 4:9). Understanding the biblical definition of hospitality as loving strangers and meeting the needs of others is critical to the success of practicing hospitality (Heb.12:1–2). Embracing a biblical definition of hospitality prevents us from becoming "Christian event planners." It also alleviates much of the pressure we often feel while extending hospitality because *biblical* hospitality is simply "love in action."[17] The hospitality we extend toward others is precious in God's sight and will be rewarded (Prov. 12:14; Matt. 10:42; Heb. 6:10). A fitting conclusion to this chapter are these words: "Whoever despises his neighbor is a sinner, but blessed is he who is generous to the poor" (Prov. 14:21).

Finally, the most important consideration is that hospitality is a reflection of God's nature. God is a welcoming God. He pursues and extends relationship, meeting needs and providing safety. As we model a life of invitation, employing our resources to meet the needs of others, we provide the world with a picture of a much greater spiritual truth—God invites all to his safe embrace.

TABLE 2.1

Examples of Old Testament Commands for Caring for the Needy

Guidelines for Caring for People	Scripture Passages	Summary of Principles
Duty to *strangers* (or aliens)	Exodus 12:48; 22:21; Leviticus 17:8; 19:34; 24:16; 25:35; Deuteronomy 5:14; 27:19; 31:12.	• Treat strangers as equals. Apply the law to *both* the native born and the alien (without distinction). • Do not mistreat strangers in any way. • The man who mistreated strangers was cursed.
Care for *widows*	Exodus 22:22; Deuteronomy 10:18; 14:29; 24:17; 26:12; Psalm 146:9; Isaiah 1:17.	• Do not take advantage of widows (or orphans). • Remember the Lord redeemed his people (from Egypt); provide for widows and orphans in the same way.
Provision for *orphans*	Deuteronomy 10:18; Psalms 10:14; 68:5; 146:9; Proverbs 15:25; 23:10; Jeremiah 49:11; Hosea 14:3.	• Defend the fatherless. • God himself is the helper of the fatherless. • Justice was commanded toward orphans.
Meeting the needs of the *poor*	Leviticus 19:10; 23:22; Deuteronomy 15:4, 11; 24:12; Psalms 34:6; 68:10; 82:3; Proverbs 13:7; 17:5; 19:1, 17; 21:13; 28:27.	• Treat the poor as you would like to be treated. • Be "openhanded" toward the poor and needy. • God will provide for your needs.
Justice commanded	Exodus 23:6; Deuteronomy 16:19; 27:19; Psalms 33:5; 72:2; 82:13; 106:3; 140:12; Proverbs 18:5; 28:5; 29:7; Jeremiah 22:16.	• Do not deny justice to the poor or needy. • The Lord loves justice. • Righteous people care about justice.
Kindness expected	Exodus 23:11; Deuteronomy 15:7; Psalm 41:1; Proverbs 19:17.	• Provide for the poor (food). • Do not be hardhearted or tightfisted with those in need. • Blessed are those who are kind to the weak. • He who is kind to the poor, lends to the Lord, and the Lord will reward him.

Practicing Hospitality

1. Write a personal definition of hospitality. Review key Scriptures to guide your thoughts and support your explanation (Rom. 12:13; Heb. 13:1–2; and 1 Pet. 4:9).

2. How do you practically show brotherly love, and why is this significant for us as Christian women to demonstrate? How can you show sisterly love? Consider Scripture (Rom. 12:10; 1 Cor. 13:4; Eph. 4:32; Col. 3:12; 2 Pet. 1:5–7).

3. What is your duty toward loving your neighbors, strangers, and enemies? Use the following chart to answer this question.

	Scripture Principles	Application
Neighbors	Mark 12:31; Romans 13:10; 15:1; Galatians 5:14; James 2:8.	
Strangers	Deuteronomy 27:19; Matthew 25:35; Hebrews 13:1–2.	
Enemies	Proverbs 24:17; 25:21–22; Matthew 5:24; Romans 12:20.	

4. If you are unfamiliar with the rich theological truths found in Romans 1–11, take some time to familiarize yourself with the amazing grace of God. Once you see the context for the command to pursue hospitality (Rom. 12:13), consider the following questions:

   - Do I reflect my gratitude for God's love for me by how I love others?
   - Do I enthusiastically pursue hospitality?
   - Do I sacrifice for the needs of others?
   - Do I model God's love through hospitality?

5. You are commanded to practice hospitality without complaining (1 Pet. 4:9). How can you personally practice hospitality "without grumbling"? List several application ideas. What hinders you from practicing hospitality? What

changes do you need to make to eliminate these barriers to hospitality?

Recipe Resources

We spent much of the chapter reflecting on the biblical definition of hospitality. In light of this, make a meal for your family using recipes that are similar to the food used during Bible times. For example, make a lentil soup, challah (braided egg bread), Mast va Khiar (cucumber and yogurt salad), and honey cake for dessert. During the meal time discuss with your family the meaning of biblical hospitality. Identify ways your family can practically demonstrate hospitality.

Lentil Soup

3 cups sliced onions
⅓ cup olive oil
¾ pound ground lamb
2½ cups canned whole tomatoes, mashed slightly
1 cup diced celery
¾ cup diced carrots
¾ cup diced parsnips
¾ cup diced green pepper
3½ cups cold water
1 pound lentils
1 tablespoon salt
½ teaspoon pepper

In Dutch oven or saucepan, sauté onions in oil until browned. Add ground lamb and cook until lamb loses its pink color. Add tomatoes, celery, carrots, parsnips, green pepper, water, lentils, and seasonings. Bring to a boil. Reduce heat and cover pan. Simmer soup about 1½ hours or until lentils are tender.

Serves 6 to 8

Challah
(Braided Egg Bread)

4½ to 5½ cups unsifted all-purpose flour
2 tablespoons sugar
1½ teaspoons salt
1 package active dry yeast
⅓ cup softened butter
Pinch powdered saffron (optional)
1 cup very warm water (120 to 130 degrees)
4 eggs (at room temperature), slightly beaten
1 teaspoon cold water
1 teaspoon poppy seeds

In large mixing bowl, combine 1¼ cups flour, sugar, salt, and dry yeast. Work in softened butter with pastry blender or two knives. Dissolve saffron in the very warm water and gradually add to dry ingredients beating on medium speed of electric mixer for 2 minutes, scraping bowl occasionally. Stir in enough additional flour to form a stiff dough. Turn dough out onto a lightly floured board or pastry cloth. Knead until smooth and elastic, about 8 to 10 minutes. Place in greased bowl, turning once to grease top. Cover with a clean towel and let rise in a warm place until doubled in bulk, about 1 hour.

Punch down. Divide dough in half; divide each half into strips (3 at a time) side by side on a lightly greased baking sheet. Beginning at the center, braid outward to edges. Seal edges well. Braid the second loaf.

Beat together reserved egg yolk with 1 teaspoon cold water. Brush loaves with egg wash and sprinkle with poppy seeds. Let rise in a warm place until doubled in bulk, about 1 hour.

Bake at 400 degrees for 20–25 minutes or until loaves sound hollow when tapped. Remove loaves from baking sheets and place on cooling racks.

Makes 2 loaves

Mast va Khiar
(Cucumber and Yogurt Salad)

2 medium cucumbers
4 tablespoons finely chopped green pepper
3 tablespoons finely chopped green onion
2 tablespoons dried tarragon or dill
1 teaspoon lime juice
½ teaspoon salt
2 cups plain yogurt

Wash cucumbers and peel. Slice each cucumber in half lengthwise. Scoop out seeds, and chop cucumber coarsely. Put cucumber in a deep bowl and add green pepper, green onion, tarragon or dill, lime juice, and salt. Mix well. Add yogurt and stir to coat vegetables. Chill at least one hour before serving.

Serves 8

Honey Cake

2 tablespoons canola oil
1 cup sugar
3 eggs
⅔ cup cold strong coffee
1 cup honey
3 cups cake flour, sifted
2 teaspoons baking powder

1 teaspoon baking soda
1 teaspoon cinnamon
½ teaspoon ginger
½ teaspoon nutmeg
½ cup blanched almonds, chopped (reserve a few for the
   top)
½ cup seedless raisins

Preheat oven to 350 degrees. In large mixing bowl, combine
oil, sugar, and eggs. Beat until light and fluffy. In small bowl,
combine coffee and honey.

Sift dry ingredients together. Add dry ingredients alternately
with liquid ingredients to egg mixture. Fold in almonds and
raisins. Pour batter into a greased and floured 9-inch tube
pan. Sprinkle batter with the reserved almonds.

Bake for 45 minutes to 1 hour, or until toothpick inserted in
center comes out clean.

Serves 10 to 12

3

Hospitality and FAMILY

Her children rise up and call her blessed; her husband also, and he praises her: "Many women have done excellently, but you surpass them all." Charm is deceitful, and beauty is vain, but a woman who fears the Lord is to be praised. Give her of the fruit of her hands, and let her works praise her in the gates.

—PROVERBS 31:28–31

For a wife and mother it is often challenging to balance the biblical mandate of practicing hospitality with the priority of meeting the needs of her family. Perhaps you too can relate to this tension. While the ministry of hospitality often focuses on those outside our home, it should begin

73

within our home. If this occurs, generosity and kindness extended to others become an extension of our family hospitality. We see this modeled in the example of the Proverbs 31 woman. She fed, clothed, and managed her household before extending her hand to the poor and needy (Prov. 31:10–31). The needs of her own family were met before she journeyed out into her community.

Family First

"She looks well to the ways of her household and does not eat the bread of idleness" (Prov. 31:27). If the Lord has given us a family, extending hospitality to our family is our first priority. Once we have established the ministry of hospitality within our family, we can then broaden our hospitality to include extended family members, friends, strangers, the needy, and the poor. Hospitality towards others then becomes a natural outworking or extension of what we are already practicing within our own homes. Why is this principle important? There are three reasons why we should consider *family first* when practicing hospitality:

1. *For the sake of our integrity.* Neglecting to extend hospitality to our family can result in violating our God-given priorities—loving our husband and children. Scripture calls us to a have a devoted affection for them. If we do not love our family as God has instructed, we can bring *dishonor* to God's Word (Titus 2:3–5). Integrity calls us to be honest and sincere in all aspects of our life. To model hospitality to the world and neglect to practice it in our own home is hypocrisy, and our integrity is compromised.
2. *For the sake of our children.* Neglecting to include our children in hospitality opportunities might create resentment in them. If our children feel unloved, abandoned, or ignored while we diligently extend hospitality

to friends and strangers, we have opened the door for developing bitterness and animosity toward hospitality in the hearts of our children. This is the opposite of what we desire to model for them when we practice hospitality. We must make our children our priority and invest the necessary time and energy to nurture and train them on a daily basis (Ps. 127:3; Prov. 22:6). How tragic for our children to loathe hospitality because they have felt a lack of care while we ministered to others. Dorothy Patterson provides a fitting reminder for mothers:

> Busyness is not godliness. God is not impressed with your production capacity as much as He is concerned that the product of your home—your own children—be chiseled and molded and perfected to the best of your ability. You may tire of this mundane task, but the Lord admonishes you not to grow weary and promises to supply the energy and strength as needed in this all-important task (Isa. 40:28–31). God's strength is for what He plans for you to do—not stamina for everything you might want to do![1]

3. *For the sake of the gospel.* Neglecting to extend hospitality to our family can discredit our witness. The testimony of a wife and mom who loves and serves her family is a powerful witness to a watching world; it is also something that separates a believing woman from the world. The manner in which we serve and love our family should reflect the transforming power of the gospel in our own life (2 Cor. 5:17–21). In other words, our love, dedication, and other biblical character attributes manifested toward our family are a testimony to the world of God's powerful work in our lives. In her book *Feminine Appeal*, Carolyn Mahaney explains the power of this witness:

75

Can you conceive of anything that sets forth the beauty of the gospel jewel more brilliantly than the godly behavior of those who have received it? Consider the loveliness of a woman who passionately adores her husband, who tenderly cherishes her children, who creates a warm and peaceful home, who exemplifies purity, self-control, and kindness in her character and who gladly submits to her husband's leadership—for all the days God grants her life. I dare say there are few things that display the gospel jewel with greater elegance.[2]

We must be diligent in protecting the priority of our family while at the same time endeavoring to be faithful to *practice hospitality* (Rom. 12:13).

Practicing Hospitality with a Family

"House and wealth are inherited from fathers, but a prudent wife is from the LORD" (Prov. 19:14). How do we keep our family a priority in the midst of reaching out to those who are in need *outside* our homes? This question is not easy to answer. Every family has unique characteristics and circumstances—family size, health conditions, financial resources, educational choices, ministry obligations, and employment requirements. There is not a single answer to fit all family types. Therefore, prudence and discernment are essential attributes for protecting the priority of our family while ministering to the needs of others.

A prudent woman acts sensibly to discern the consequences of her choices, for example, in how a particular hospitality event will impact her time, energy, and family. A discerning woman is one who uses good judgment in her choices. Prudence and discernment working together allow us to make wise choices with our time, energy, and resources.

Proverbs 8:12 states, "I, wisdom, dwell with prudence and I find knowledge and discretion."

Every woman will need to evaluate her own unique family constraints and then develop strategies to assist her in promoting the welfare of her family, while at the same time allowing her to participate in the rich ministry of hospitality with people who are not in her immediate family. There are several helpful principles to consider.

Principle One: Remember there are seasons in life. There will be seasons in our lives when we will be able to spend more or less time practicing hospitality. For example, when I was newly married with no children, I had much more time and energy to give to hospitality. I would prepare homemade dinners for large groups of people, meet friends for lunch, and participate in various ministry events outside my home. Now that I am married and the mother of five children, I often purchase food for large groups from local restaurants, dovetail meeting friends with trips to the park while my children play, and limit my participation in events outside my home. Why? Because caring for my children is my priority during this season of life, and in order to meet their needs, I must limit my participation in other activities (including hospitality opportunities).

We can easily become frustrated with the limitations of each season in life if we do not also appreciate the opportunities each brings. Practicing hospitality can be experienced during every season of life. However, it may not always be implemented in the same manner. We may need to invite people for dessert rather than a full meal, or meet them for breakfast rather than lunch. Our commitment to hospitality should motivate us to be flexible and resourceful during each season of life.

If we do not resourcefully adjust to each season of life, the resulting frustration can easily turn to bitterness. We become discontent with our current season, potentially robbing us of the enjoyment that it can bring. During the child-raising season, sinful bitterness can cause us to view our children as inconveniences rather than as the precious gifts God intended. Scripture commands believers to "put away" all bitterness (Eph. 4:31–32). Embracing our seasons of life allows us to continue to practice hospitality joyfully with creative flexibility and resourcefulness, while at the same time maintaining our God-given priorities.

Principle Two: Partner with your husband. Women readily think that hospitality is their responsibility alone. While it is true that most wives, as "keepers of the home," will oversee and organize many of the details related to hospitality, Scripture calls *all* believers to be hospitable. Scripture identifies being hospitable as a qualification for men who will be leaders in the churches (1 Tim. 1:8; 3:2). Likewise, men are called to lead and love their families in all areas. Wives should let their husbands set the tone for hospitality for their families—both within their homes and with others. There are three primary benefits in working together with your husband.

First, your husband can give you counsel and direction regarding how much time you can dedicate to hospitality. You should be eager to receive counsel from your husband, as this Scripture states: "Without counsel plans fail, but with many advisors they succeed" (Prov. 15:22). The protection of working under the authority of your husband is a blessing, since he knows your physical limitations, work or ministry responsibilities, and unique family characteristics. Your husband will be able to assist you in making wise decisions regarding how you use your time and energy.

Partnering with your husband brings a more balanced perspective to hospitality within your home. Peggy Rowan provides a good illustration for this principle:

> Because of Dave's (my husband's) upbringing in Brazil, he was much more hospitable than I was. Brazilians don't mind dropping in unannounced; therefore Dave didn't mind inviting people in all the time. He has learned that I need more privacy so he consults me before asking people over. I have

learned to "just do it" (show hospitality) and not talk myself out of having people over because of all my insecurities. Because Dave grew up in a missionary family, they didn't have much money and neither did the people they lived among, so Dave has always been hospitable whether we have lived below the poverty level or been financially comfortable. That has helped me not to think I have to have all sorts of stuff to make people comfortable.[3]

Third, your husband can help with the work and preparations; sharing the responsibility allows both of you to exercise your unique giftedness. Practicing hospitality with a family requires teamwork. Your husband can lovingly lead and guide the family into hospitality ministry opportunities, and you can function as the facilitator of hospitality in your home.

Principle Three: Include your children. When I am busy preparing to entertain and receive guests into my home, I can easily become focused on my list of tasks—grocery shopping, cleaning the house, and food preparation. I can become frustrated with my children because I begin to view them as interruptions keeping me from accomplishing my list of tasks rather than seeing them as the priority for my time and energy. As I mentioned earlier, neglecting to include my children in the process of hospitality can plant seeds of bitterness in their hearts—they will not be excited about reaching out to meet the needs of others. Additionally, it robs them of valuable life lessons and learning experiences. For example, as Tammi Schmorleitz points out, "We include the whole family so the kids of another family feel welcome too. It's good practice for my kids to be able to welcome kids they don't know into their rooms and to share their toys."[4] Three simple strategies help me remember that my children are more important than the preparations for an event.

First, *I look for ways to include my children in the preparations*. If your children are like mine, they are eager helpers and always excited to participate in the preparations. However, I have to look for creative ways to include them. While it is always easier and faster to do tasks myself, I deprive my children of valuable life skills and lose precious teachable moments by excluding them. Can they help plan the menu? Set the table or make a table centerpiece? Mix the cookie dough or decorate the cake? Color a picture for the guests? There are usually several ways even my youngest child can help if I intentionally look for ways to include him.

Second, *I allow extra time for tasks*. There is no way around this one—including children takes more time and is often more work. However, the benefits are well worth it. Deuteronomy 6:4–9 admonishes us to teach our children diligently while we talk, walk, sit, lie down, and rise up. Training our children occurs in the midst of life—including when we are preparing to extend hospitality. By planning ahead and anticipating that tasks will take longer, we allow for training time.

Third, *I am willing to set aside my "to do" list* for the needs of my children. The needs of my children vary. Some days they need a band-aid and a hug after a fall on the sidewalk; other days require time for discipline issues, while others simply a few minutes of playtime together. Whatever the need, the common thread is my time. My children should never be viewed as interruptions or inconveniences. Since they are gifts we have only for a season in life, we should strive to be faithful stewards with the treasure God has entrusted to our care (Ps. 127:3).

Principle Four: Treat your family "as good as guests." Often we treat our guests better than our family. Establishing the habit of treating our family as we would a guest will assist us in communicating our love to our family. Extending hospitality to our family allows them to reap the same blessings our guests receive in our home. Also, we are modeling for our children how to honor guests—they learn from our example. Treating our family as guests also reinforces the concept of family first. Below are some simple ideas to practice hospitality with your family.

Prepare their favorite foods. Use food to honor a family member for a special occasion like a birthday or at the time of a significant accomplishment. I have a friend who also uses a plate inscribed with "You Are Special" to honor her family members.

Set the table. It is easy to get in the habit of using paper plates and plastic cups; however, setting the table with china, a nice tablecloth, and fresh cut flowers creates a completely different atmosphere in your home, communicating to your husband and children that you have given thought to the preparation of the meal and are joyful about serving them.

Check your appearance! Do you change your clothes, touch up your makeup, or comb your hair before your guests arrive? I usually do. Why, then, do we not give our spouse the same courtesy? I learned this lesson from my mother when I was eight or nine years old. Late one afternoon I wandered into my mother's room and found her putting on lipstick and combing her hair. I asked her where she was going, and her response was, "Nowhere; your father will be home from work soon." She made a vivid impression on me that day and taught me an important lesson—Dad was important to her, and one way she communicated that was by how she cared for herself. While we should not be overly consumed with our physical appearance, maintaining our appearance out of love for our spouse is appropriate. Consider how you looked when you were dating—do you maintain the same degree of physical appearance?

Create a warm atmosphere. We endeavor to create a peaceful environment for guests, and we can do the same for our family. Simple things like turning on music and lighting candles will create a restful ambience for our family to enjoy. We can create an environment that encourages conversation around the dinner table long after the meal is eaten.

Screen your phone calls. If your telephone rings while you have guests in your home, you can let the answering machine take a message or you can ask the caller if you can return the call at a later time. Then you are able to give your attention and time to your guests. Why not do the same thing for your family? Screen your phone calls or simply do not answer the phone during designated family time. You are then free to focus on greeting your children after school or your husband after work. You protect the limited family time you enjoy in the evenings, and you help facilitate time for uninterrupted family activities—conversation, devotion or prayer time, and fun activities like playing games. Patti Morse shares how she practices this principle: "This may sound silly, but ten minutes before either one of my children or my husband is to return home from school and work, I do not answer the telephone. I screen all calls, so I can be ready to greet my loved one at the door with a hug and my undivided attention."[5]

Plan special events. You can make any day or meal a special occasion simply by investing some time planning ahead. Special events do not need to be elaborate in scope or cost to be meaningful. Eat outside by candlelight on your patio, prepare a picnic dinner for a summer concert at the park, have a popcorn and movie night, make a dessert (especially if desserts are usually reserved for guests), or decorate your table to reflect a theme for the meal. Select a children's theme (themes used in my home include cowboys and Indians, trains, and teddy bears) or prepare ethnic foods and then decorate to match the culture (Chinese, Mexican, or Italian). Laurie Twibell explains how she practices this in her home:

> We usually have Mexican food on Thursdays, and I've made a hot pepper tablecloth and bought Mexican dishes to use. I've also bought some plates to use with Italian food. I had gone the route of plain dishes and a variety of tablecloths but that got boring after a while, so I'm always on the lookout for four unique, cheap plates to buy for my family. It's very easy to treat guests as more special than my own husband and children so I consciously work against that.[6]

Principle Five: Keep an orderly home. You probably spend time cleaning the house *before* guests arrive; however, do you clean *after* they leave? We will see in chapter 4 that one of the main reasons to manage our home is for the sake of hospitality. We should also consider managing our home for the sake of hospitality to our family. Cleaning and organizing is a part of the practical outworking of Titus 2:3–5. Keeping an orderly home communicates our love in a tangible manner. Our family benefits from our management on a daily basis, just as guests enjoy our efforts when they visit.[7]

Principle Six: Use discretion. Practicing hospitality with family requires wise decisions for their safety and well-being. Discretion implies that we are careful and exercise wise caution. Compassionate women are vulnerable in a sinful world. "The simple believes everything, but the prudent gives thought to his steps" (Prov. 14:15). We should be careful to exercise discernment with strangers and attempt to make wise decisions that allow us to be involved with meeting the needs of others while also considering the welfare of our family. How do you balance serving others while considering the well-being of your family? Below are a few ideas.

- Discuss with your husband appropriate parameters for inviting people into your home. You may decide that it is acceptable to bring strangers home when you are both present but not when you are home alone with your children.
- Participate in your local church outreach programs to meet the needs of special groups of people. Crisis pregnancy centers, homeless shelters, and hospital visitation all provide wonderful opportunities to practice hospitality.
- Locate Christian para-church organizations that specialize in ministering to needy people such as food pantries or transitional care homes.

- Work with local community-based programs that allow you to meet the needs of your neighborhood, for example, teaching life skills to emancipated minors from the foster care system (nutrition, cooking, finances, consumer shopping skills) or participating in new immigrant training programs.

Ultimately you must commend the safety of your family to the Lord and trust his provision in the midst of ministering to strangers and needy people.

Principle Seven: Remember meaningful moments. The final principle for extending hospitality to our family is to become the keeper of memories in our home. Part of building our family bond will include remembering the significant and fun times shared together. Without intentional efforts to remember, we easily forget cherished moments. Practicing hospitality with and toward your family will provide numerous opportunities to build your relationships.

There are a variety of ways to remember, including taking photos or videos of special events and creating scrapbooks or photo albums of family vacations or birthdays, holidays, and weddings. You can establish other traditions that allow you to remember, such as writing letters to commemorate family events and then placing them in a notebook, creating a family journal of significant memories. Another great way to treasure memories is to establish unique family traditions. Why are traditions important? Traditions create strong memories in the lives of our family members. Here are a few practical suggestions to get you started.

Family Traditions

"Remember also your Creator in the days of your youth, before the evil days come and the years draw near of which you will say, 'I have no pleasure in them'" (Eccles. 12:1).

Practicing hospitality with your family provides a wonderful opportunity to create meaningful memories through family traditions. What is a tradition? A *tradition* can be defined as "the handing down of beliefs, opinions, customs, stories, etc., from parents to children."[8] Traditions influence both our thoughts and practices. Traditions are the *heritage* we pass down from one generation to the next.[9]

Most women would agree that establishing family traditions benefits a family, but at the same time women experience various challenges in implementing meaningful practices. There are also numerous questions related to traditions—what is the motivation for establishing traditions or why should we establish them? How do we establish traditions? What are the benefits to our family? Let's consider the *importance*, the *interpretation*, and the *influence* of family traditions.

The Importance of Family Traditions

There are several reasons *why* we should consider establishing family traditions. First, *family traditions provide a sense of stability or permanence in our homes*. Life is full of change, adjustments, and new experiences. Family traditions allow us to provide a sense of steadiness or constancy in our family. Traditions can create a sanctuary for our family that remains constant regardless of changing life circumstances—changes in employment, school, health, or residence location. Dorothy Patterson explains this principle very well:

> The home should be a haven where familiar traditions and rituals reassure its residents that life, even with its turmoil and difficulties, is indeed worth the effort. Those traditions that make your family unique will go with you wherever you travel and be the human rock to which you can cling. Home should be a source for gathering strength for the challenges of life, a living album for remembering the past and your heritage, an

oasis for finding joy to celebrate the present moment, and a reservoir of energy and optimism that enables you to recharge your batteries to go out into the future highways of life.[10]

Second, *family traditions provide a method for remembering God's work in our lives.* Memories are wonderful gifts from God. As believers, we can utilize memories to commemorate God's sovereign work in our lives. As Psalm 119:55 says, "I remember your name in the night, O LORD, and keep your law." The principle of *remembering* is clearly seen in Scripture. Here are just a few examples:

- Guidelines for ceremonies that remember God's deliverance (Lev. 23:42–43; Est. 9:20–32).
- Commands to establish feasts or celebrations to remember God's mercy (Exodus 12). Directives to set up memorial stones to remember God's faithfulness (Josh. 4:1–7).
- Instructions to teach children so they do not forget God's acts (Ex. 12:16–27; Deut. 4:9–10; 6:4–10).
- General directives throughout Scripture to remember God and his power or works (Deut. 8:18; Neh. 4:14; Eccles. 12:1).

The principle of remembering is important for us to apply; meaningful traditions help our family *remember* God's work in our lives.

Third, *family traditions provide a means for passing on a godly heritage to our children.* For believers, family traditions provide a wonderful opportunity to reinforce biblical truths in their hearts and in the lives of their children. Noël Piper, in her book *Treasuring God in Our Traditions*, explains this principle well: "For a Christian, tradition is laying up God's words in our own hearts and passing his words to the next generation."[11] This definition implies that traditions are not just for the benefit of our children but for the whole family, when they are focused on God's

Word. Traditions based on teaching God's attributes, laws, or wisdom result in creating meaningful traditions rather than purposeless rituals.

The Interpretation of Family Traditions

If establishing family traditions is a worthy pursuit, how can you create meaningful traditions in your home? Most women desire to establish traditions, but many neglect to invest the time needed to establish intentional, thoughtful, and purposeful traditions. There are three areas to consider as you pass on a heritage to your family: a spiritual heritage, a kindred heritage, and a holiday heritage.

1) A Spiritual Heritage

The priority for believers should be establishing family traditions that provide a method for passing on biblical truths about God, his Word, and their personal relationship with him. Spiritual traditions should not be confused with meaningless rituals; rather, they are a means whereby parents can model for their children a dynamic Christian life by allowing their children to observe their practices and attitudes regarding spiritual issues. For example, you can pass on a spiritual heritage by modeling worship, prayer, individual devotions, Scripture memory, church participation, and biblical principles for relationships, such as practicing hospitality in your home. Here are a few ideas from friends, my own home, and our survey participants to get you started:

- Practice family devotions together (read the Word, pray, and sing together as a family).
- Exercise hospitality as a family (prepare extra food on Sundays in anticipation of inviting visitors home from church).

87

- Give to the needy (save coins, donate used clothes or household items, participate in toy drives).
- Throw birthday parties with a purpose. Have your party guests bring toys, food, or clothing to be donated to a local charity instead of presents for your children. Have your child help you deliver them to the organization of your choice. Maximize this "teachable moment."
- Serve others as a family by doing volunteer work (preparing meals, mowing lawns, babysitting, visiting the elderly).
- Elizabeth Gilbert comments, "In our own home one thing we practice for sure is a regular daily Bible reading with discussion. I take the children through a psalm and a proverb each day along with the memorization of one chapter of the Bible a month, many picked from the Psalms. We try to incorporate the Scripture throughout the day and at all teachable moments. We try to abide by Deuteronomy 6:7–9. A practice in our home more recently is to play melodious, worshipful music. It seems to help to create a calmer and more peaceful atmosphere, which is something we definitely support."
- Heather Lanker says that her family goes to her parents' home on Sundays after church where they all eat dinner together. They read their children Bible stories every morning at breakfast and pray with their children at bedtime.
- Debby Lennick uses her home by regularly opening it to friends, family, and even newly acquainted brothers and sisters in Christ and offers this example: "This last summer my oldest daughter, who works in our church's Urban Ministries program, wanted to have her office staff over weekly for dinner. The purpose was to build unity and kinship among those who work in this office. It was a wonderful time of fellowship for them and our family. And she even did the cooking!"

2) A Kindred Heritage

Unique family characteristics and calendar dates distinctive to your family can be used to build unity. Birthdays, anniversaries, weddings, deaths, and other unique dates (for example, adoption dates) can all be celebrated through memorable family traditions. A few suggestions to get you started include:

- Write letters to include with a gift to family members celebrating growth in their character on birthdays or other special dates (Mother's Day or Father's Day, anniversaries).
- Call your family members not only on the day they were born, but also at the exact time they were born (even if it is in the middle of the night!).
- Look at your children's baby books or family photo albums on their birthday; rehearse the year's events acknowledging God's blessings.
- Plant a tree to mark family events (births, deaths, or anniversaries).
- Vicki Ferretti says that traditions that support her marriage are date night and saying goodnight to one another in the same words on a daily basis. "Now that I am home full time, I make it a priority to have dinner ready when Bryan gets home from work to ensure healthful eating when we are both hungry instead of snacking. With a child, money must stretch even further so I try to think of a weekly fun day that is free or inexpensive. These special days shared as a family build memories as well as relationships. For example, last Monday (my husband's day off), we went to Golden Gate Park to feed the ducks, walk around the lake, and swing on the swings. We spent ten dollars on hot dogs and popcorn for lunch and had a very special day. I'll never forget it."

- Elizabeth Gilbert states, "Mom is into pleasing Dad. When he is home in the morning we have a special breakfast that includes waffles. As a tradition passed down from her family, Mom prepares the waffles adding extra interesting ingredients that the family has to guess during breakfast. This has been more fun and supports a time of love and laughter around the table."

- Erin McLeod uses a "You Are Special" plate, which is given to a family member on his birthday, after a big accomplishment, or just "because." She plans lots of "family parties to celebrate various occasions around the holidays, for neighbors and friends; special notes to remind each other of your love; cake and ice cream for breakfast on the morning of each family member's birthday; date nights with my husband, special desserts or treats to celebrate a job well done or just to celebrate being together."

- Robin Contreras shares, "My husband enjoys meats in his breakfast meals, so I'm trying to start a tradition of breakfast that includes even chicken or red meat in breakfast enchiladas."

- Patti Morse suggests, "Hospitality begins with your own family members." She has several fun ideas:

  - Every Friday night is a special night with a fun theme dictating the meal and decorations. It is always a surprise to my family ("Under the Sea Night," "Fiesta Night," or "Train Wreck Night").

  - I never have a family dinner without including something special in my preparations—special china, a special location, special music, special candles, a new dish, or special notes at each setting.

  - Birthdays must also be accompanied by at least one unexpected surprise sometime during the day.

- We try to have one new family over for dinner each month and plan a fun evening of food and fellowship.
- We never allow family or friends to leave without first asking them how we can pray for them throughout the week.
- Traditionally, our home is known as the "Morse Motel" where there is always an open door with a "Morse buffet" ready and waiting. I would not have it any other way! I always make sure there are clean linens on the guest bed, lots of extra blankets for the sofas and floors, and plenty of prepared food in the refrigerator/freezer.

• Kelli Gleeson describes the traditions she and her husband started when they married: "Every year, we take off work the day of our anniversary. It's such a special day, one that we want to hold in high regard, the day we committed our lives to one another and to God's work as a couple."

• Anne Goad shares, "We have family meals. Every morning (almost!) we read the Bible and pray. We go to our Christmas Eve service. I have sung my girls to sleep every night since they were born with praise and worship songs. We have fun birthdays. My husband and I have a date every week. We try to go on an overnight for a getaway every few months (just the two of us)."

3) A Holiday Heritage

There are numerous religious or cultural holidays from which to choose when establishing family traditions. Both provide us with the opportunity to create significant memories for our families to look forward to each time the seasons change. A few ideas include:

- Preparing the same food item for each holiday—cinnamon rolls for Thanksgiving, iced sugar cookies for Christmas, or deviled eggs for Easter.
- New Year's Eve Blessings Box—fill a file box with blank cards; throughout the year write significant events, blessings, or lessons learned and read the cards with your family on New Year's Eve.
- Make a birthday cake for Jesus on Christmas Day.
- Use place cards at meals with Scripture verses on them celebrating the holiday, verses about Christmas or Easter, or verses about the holiday theme, such as love or thanksgiving.
- Angi Roe says, "On holidays we often invite several of the military families in our area that don't have other family around. It has been special to share our time with others."
- Robin Contreras celebrates "Thanksgiving with both sides of our family, if possible, or with other missionaries here in Mexico, and we celebrate Christmas the night before Christmas with our Mexican relatives and visit with others the next day. We also want to celebrate Mexican Independence Day with friends from church (in September) and have celebrated Day of the Wise Men in January with the traditional eating of a special cake."
- Lisa DiGiacomo shares that each Christmas she and her husband "give each daughter a Christmas ornament all their own, which they hang on our Christmas tree. Oftentimes the ornament reflects something they learned how to do that year or that they enjoyed doing. When they leave our home, we will give them these ornaments to put upon their own Christmas tree. My mother did this for me and it was very special."
- Kelli Gleeson says that at Christmas, "We set aside either Christmas morning or Christmas Eve (depending which side of the family we are with that year) to pray together,

read the Christmas story, and *really* remember why we are celebrating this amazing holiday. Then we open our gifts with a heart of gratitude, understanding the one true gift of Jesus Christ."

The Influence of Family Traditions

While each family will establish its own unique set of family traditions, the influences on the family will have common characteristics:

- fostering stability and security by establishing routines;
- emphasizing God's sovereign work in our family;
- building a strong family bond through time invested in relationships;
- creating priceless family memories; and
- modeling biblical practices and attitudes about God and his Word.

Traditions are a wonderful tool you can use to pass on a strong spiritual, kindred, and holiday heritage. They can be both meaningful and fun. Ledbetter and Smith remind us:

> Traditions are the family's God-ordained vehicle to pass on a positive heritage. It doesn't cost a lot of money to pass on valuable traditions. But it will cost time, thinking, and the courage to move from ideas to action.[12]

A Concluding Consideration

This chapter has emphasized the priority of family first, has given ideas for implementing hospitality with a family, and has suggested ways to create meaningful traditions to pass on a godly heritage to our children. There is one final consideration—the importance of time alone as a family. There is a delicate balance between having an open-door policy and knowing when we should close the door for the sake of our family. Your family will profit from:

- time alone for each family member to commune with God and renew his or her spiritual strength;
- time alone with your spouse to talk, pray, and encourage each other;
- time alone with your children to train, teach, and understand their heart issues; and
- time alone as a family to build relationships and strengthen your family bond.

Time alone will become the backbone for practicing hospitality and sharing your family with others. In her book *What Is a Family?* Edith Schaeffer describes hospitality as being a door with both hinges and a lock. Consider her words of advice:

A family is a door that has hinges and a lock. The hinges should be well-oiled to swing the door open during certain times, but the lock should be firm enough to let people know that the family needs to be alone part of the time, just to be a family. If a family is to be really shared, then there needs to be something to share. Whatever we share needs time for preparation. If we are going to share bread we need to be provided with the flour, eggs, yeast, sugar, milk, and whatever else we might put in it, and we need to have time to make the dough and bake it before it can be shared. If we took flour, sugar, a cake of yeast, some milk or water, and an egg or two, and tossed them out the window for someone begging for bread, a nasty mess would fall at his feet in a form that would do him no good.

It seems that there is a danger of having a door so open that there might just as well not be walls, so that there is no shelter at all to enter. In the same way, the family to be shared can also be in a state of just being raw, scattered ingredients of a family, which need time to become the "bread" which could be helpful to the hungry on needing the reality of a family to share. The kneading and molding and mixing and blending are things which go on throughout a lifetime of putting a family together, but if a certain amount of the togetherness of the ingredients has not taken place, there is nothing at all to share, and the one seeking help comes to an "empty table."[13]

Edith Schaeffer also said:

> We can't have any of the realities of what a family can be without the Lord's help, and we certainly can't have the reality of a family as an open door with hinges and a lock, without constantly praying that the Lord will help us to be ready for the ones whom He sends. Yet we are not presumptuously to plunge into sharing what we don't have to share. There is a delicate balance here, of willingness to sacrifice the praise of others for being "so wonderfully open," when we are meant to be giving privacy to each other, to our children, and to the Lord Himself.[14]

May God grant you the wisdom (James 1:5) to lovingly nurture your family through the ministry of hospitality, while at the same time balancing the mandate to reach out to needy people in your neighborhood, community, and, ultimately, the world (James 1:23–27).

Practicing Hospitality

1. Are you thankful or bitter about your current season in life? Review the Scriptures below to evaluate if your heart is truly thankful or if bitterness has developed toward your family or life circumstances.

Scripture References	Principles to Apply
Bitterness	
Proverbs 14:10	
Ephesians 4:31	
Colossians 3:8	
Hebrews 12:14–15	
Thankfulness	
Psalm 28:7	
Psalm 92:1	
Romans 6:17–18	
1 Thessalonians 5:18	

2. Do you practice hospitality to your family? Evaluate whether you treat your family "as good as guests." Identify how you can specifically apply the ideas mentioned in this chapter.

- I can prepare favorite foods by serving_____.
- I can set the table using_____.
- I can give attention to my appearance by_____.
- I can create a warm atmosphere by_____.
- I can screen phone calls or other interruptions by _____.
- I can plan special events by_____.

3. Take time to tell your family they are a priority in your life. Write a short letter to your spouse and each child communicating your heart's desire to keep your family first. You might want to:

- communicate your devotion and affection;
- affirm their character;
- rehearse favorite memories stored in your heart;
- share your prayers for their lives;
- identify why you are thankful God placed them in your family.

4. Begin practicing family traditions. If you are married, consult your spouse and incorporate ideas that are important to him. Use the chart below to create a list of ideas and then begin adding new traditions as the seasons change or family events occur.

Tradition Type	Ideas I Would Like to Implement
Spiritual Heritage	Example: Family devotions
Kindred Heritage	Example: Writing family members letters on their respective birthdays affirming their character
Holiday Heritage	Example: Selecting foods to serve each holiday

5. Read more about it! I would suggest starting with Noël Piper's *Treasuring God in Our Traditions*. In addition to this resource, there are numerous books filled with ideas for family traditions, such as *The Family Treasury of Great Holiday Ideas*.[15]

Recipe Resources

Traditions in my home are often associated with the food I serve. Below are several recipes I traditionally serve.

- Thanksgiving: bread machine Cinnamon Rolls (I make them the night before, allowing the dough to rise in the refrigerator overnight).
- Christmas: Mom's Iced Sugar Cookies
- Birthdays: Lemon Pound Cake

Cinnamon Rolls

1 egg plus enough water to equal 1 cup
3½ cups bread flour
1 teaspoon salt
⅓ cup sugar
¼ cup oil
1½ teaspoons yeast

Filling:
½ cup (1 stick) butter
1 cup packed brown sugar
½ cup chopped walnuts
2 tablespoons cinnamon
¼ cup raisins (optional)

Cream Cheese Frosting:
8 ounces cream cheese
½ cup butter (1 stick)

2 teaspoons vanilla
4½–4¾ cups powdered sugar (1 box)

Combine bread ingredients following bread machine directions or mix ingredients by hand and allow to rise in a warm place until the dough has doubled. Select "dough" setting (sweet dough if available). Combine filling ingredients while dough is processing.

After dough cycle, remove and roll into a 9 x 13 rectangle. Spread filling ingredients over dough. Roll up (jellyroll style) starting on shorter edge. Cut into 12 regular sized or 18 mini rolls. Allow to rise a second time until doubled in size or leave in refrigerator overnight and bake fresh in the morning.

Bake for 25–30 minutes at 350 degrees. Allow to cool 5 minutes and then frost with cream cheese frosting.

Mom's Iced Sugar Cookies

½ cup butter
1 cup sugar
2 eggs
1 teaspoon vanilla
2½ cups sifted flour
2 teaspoons baking powder
½ teaspoon salt
1 teaspoon grated lemon peel

Icing:
1 stick butter
1 box powdered sugar
½ teaspoon vanilla
pinch salt
water or milk for desired consistency

Heat oven to 375 degrees. Cream butter and sugar. Add eggs and vanilla. Mix. Add dry ingredients; blend well. Chill dough (about an hour or more). Roll out with a floured pin on a lightly floured board (or roll between wax paper). Roll ¼-inch to ⅓-inch thick. Cut into shapes using cookie cutters. Bake for 8–10 minutes or until slightly golden. Cool 1–2 minutes; remove from cookie sheet. Frost cookies with icing and decorate as desired.

Makes 3 dozen

Lemon Pound Cake

1 lemon cake mix
1 lemon instant pudding mix
½ cup oil
4 eggs
1 cup water

Glaze:
2 cups powdered sugar
4 tablespoons milk or water
1 lemon (juice)

Heat oven to 350 degrees. Mix together all ingredients. Follow baking directions on cake box. For Bundt pan bake 35–40 minutes. For glaze: stir all ingredients together. Drizzle over cake. Serves 12.

4

Hospitality
and MANAGEMENT

Whatever you do, work heartily, as for the Lord and not for men.

—COLOSSIANS 3:23

Several years ago my husband and I had the opportunity to visit Colonial Williamsburg in Virginia. As we strolled along the quaint streets reflecting on life as it was over two hundred years ago, I could not help noticing the repetitive use of the pineapple motif. It was prominently displayed on fabric prints, wall art, furniture designs, and architectural details. I discovered on our trip that the pineapple became a symbol of hospitality during Colonial times because it was a rare and exotic fruit brought to America by seafaring captains who sailed the Caribbean in and around the West Indies. They returned from their long expeditions with fruit, spices, and other cargo. The sea captain would place a pineapple on a fence post outside his home to let his friends know of his safe return. "The pineapple was an invitation for them to visit, share his food and drink, and listen to the tales of his voyage."[1] Innkeepers began to reinforce the pineapple as a symbol for hospitality by carving it on their signs to welcome travelers. This practice is still seen in the South today.

Many colonial women purchased pineapples for special occasions, and those who did were considered very resource-ful.[2] They had to plan ahead, rise early, and be one of the first to arrive at the market in order to purchase this rare fruit. Also, pineapples were expensive so serving one reflected that the hostess had sacrificed for her guests. Pineapples were usually prominently displayed as the centerpiece of elaborate table decorations.[3] They were then often served as a refreshing dessert after a multi-course meal. The hostess who offered her guests pineapple was offering her guests the very best that could be purchased at the time. Thus, the pineapple came to symbolize a gracious welcome as well as resourceful management.

The pineapple remains a traditional symbol for hospitality and is a reminder of the important role management skills have traditionally played in welcoming guests into our homes.[4] Because hospitality has been defined as serving others, it is important to consider how your management skills impact your ability to practice hospitality today. While pineapples are no longer a rare fruit, management skills are still required for a hostess to offer hospitality with graciousness and ease. Why is it especially important for the Christian woman to develop her management skills as they relate to hospitality?

The Importance of Managing

"In all toil there is profit, but mere talk tends only to poverty" (Prov. 14:23). Management skills are important for Christian women primarily because such skills are the key to extending hospitality with ease, enjoyment, and resourcefulness. A part of looking over the activities of our household (Prov. 31:27a) means we are able to organize and bring order to our homes—in other words, manage. Management helps us maximize our time, energy, and resources. Simply put, management helps us be good stewards. Likewise, management allows us to plan and organize events so we are free to focus on our real priority—people! What does it mean to manage? Hospitality management can be defined as "the ability to handle details and decisions skillfully in order to accomplish a plan or purpose; the ability to receive, entertain, and meet graciously the needs of guests in our home."[5]

Management involves organizing and planning all the details for each hospitality event. *Organizing* is the ability to arrange the various parts of your event; it implies that you are able to make decisions and accomplish tasks.[6] Planning is the process of deciding in advance how to accomplish your tasks or goals,[7] while organizing suggests you know how to implement your plans.[8]

Planning is an important part of hospitality. Without planning you will not be prepared to meet the needs of guests, and you might miss opportunities to extend hospitality. Planning suggests you are *anticipating* opportunities to prepare a meal, invite a guest to stay the night, or open your home to others in some way. It allows you to be prepared to deliver a meal to a sick friend or a new mom, bring home a visitor or a missionary after church, or include a single friend or an international student on a family outing. Any time you extend hospitality, planning is required. Unfortunately, we are often unprepared because we have not anticipated opportunities. Steve Wilkins suggests that we should be "planners of generosity":

> So we should always be ready to take advantage of opportunities to exercise hospitality. If we are to "entertain strangers,"

as the author of Hebrews says, we should be prepared for such unexpected guests. If we are ready, entertaining them is an opportunity of great pleasure instead of an occasion for panic. If we do not plan, difficulties and objections arise immediately in our minds, and it will be easy to let opportunity slip by. Any duty that involves some difficulty or trouble will seem tedious unless we remember its beauty and usefulness, having already made the necessary preparations for it. Then, when the need arises, we are ready to fulfill our duty with joy and gladness.[9]

I would encourage you to make one of your goals that of becoming a "planner of generosity." Three strategies to assist you in the planning process include: refuse idleness, manage your home, and prepare for graciousness. Giving attention to these areas may help you manage with ease and enjoyment any opportunity the Lord brings to your home.

Refuse Idleness

"She looks well to the ways of her household and does not eat the bread of idleness" (Prov. 31:27). Managing our homes with excellence will require that we are never idle. What does this mean for you as you consider managing your home in preparation for hospitality? Idleness means we are "doing nothing" or "not busy working."[10] It suggests we are lazy or slothful. Idleness implies wasted time and pictures a person who is unemployed. This picture is completely contrary to how Scripture defines a woman's responsibility to her family and home. Titus 2:5 calls women to be "workers at home."[11] They are to be "employed at home."[12] A person with integrity works hard at her place of employment, meaning she is busy with tasks, redeeming the time, and refusing idleness.

I recently had a young wife visiting me in my home, and she commented on how clean my home was and wanted to know my secret. I did not know how to respond at that time, so I simply thanked her for what I considered to be a compliment. After she left that day, I reflected on her comment many times and realized that many women really do think there is a secret to having an orderly home. However, the truth is that there is no secret to managing your home with excellence—it is simply hard work!

Consistent effort is required to have an orderly and prepared home, whereas idleness nullifies hard work. You must work diligently—every day. According to Scripture, the consequences of idleness are always disastrous:

- want (Prov. 20:4);
- poverty (Prov. 10:4; 20:13);
- hunger (Prov. 19:15);
- bondage (Prov. 12:24);
- apathy, and ruin (Prov. 24:30–34).

Refusing idleness is essential to a well-managed and orderly home. The Puritan Thomas Watson described God's disapproval of idleness: "That same God who says, 'Remember the Sabbath-day to keep it holy,' also says, 'six days shalt thou labour.' The great God never sealed any warrants for idleness."[13]

The opposite of idleness is *diligence*. Diligence suggests one who is industrious and faithful in her effort or labor. Believers are called to excel in diligence (see 2 Cor. 8:7). This means women are to exemplify or model diligence. Scripture calls the character attribute of diligence "precious wealth" (Prov. 12:27b). Are you a diligent woman or an idle woman? Proverbs 21:5 says, "The plans of the diligent lead surely to abundance, but everyone who is hasty comes only to poverty." Below are some qualities that reflect our commitment to refusing idleness and pursuing diligence.

We work hard. Our diligent work ethic reflects that we view our home as our place of employment. We should be committed to becoming skilled managers of our home as Titus 2:4–5 describes. This may require that we pursue a mentoring relationship with an older woman to learn how to work hard and manage our home with excellence.

We make a consistent effort. In my experience I rarely complete all the projects on my "to do" list in a single day (and if I did, that would be the day my children would walk through the house with muddy shoes!). There will always be work to complete. Rather than becoming discouraged by the undone tasks and giving up, I make a consistent effort—every day—to organize and manage my home (Prov. 24:33–34).

We are industrious. We cannot be lazy women and manage with excellence. Scripture often uses the term "sluggard" when referring to a lazy person (Prov. 12:27; 13:4; 26:13–16). Being a sluggard is completely opposite to the godly character God desires to see in believers (Prov. 10:4; 12:24; 13:4). The ant is contrasted to the sluggard in Proverbs 6:6–11 and serves as an example of diligence and planning. The ant works hard in the summer storing up food in anticipation for the winter. We should work hard like the ant in preparation for the needs of our family, home, and guests (Prov. 30:25–26).

Manage Your Home

"And so train the young women to love their husbands and children, to be self-controlled, pure, working at home, kind, and submissive to their own husbands, that the word of God may not be reviled" (Titus 2:4–5). The first practical step in preparation for hospitality is to *manage your home*. Why? Because a well-managed home views hospitality as a life-style—not just an event. You are living in anticipation that you will have guests in your home. A clean and orderly home allows you to receive guests at any time, without hesitation or embarrassment. Having a prepared home allows you greater freedom and flexibility in practicing hospitality; in other words, one of the reasons you keep your home organized is for *the sake of hospitality*. Steve Wilkins suggests that a disorderly and undisciplined lifestyle will be hindrances to hospitality:

> If our lives, homes, and routines are in a state of disarray, and we are hardly able to sufficiently take care of ourselves, we will naturally be discouraged from ministering to others. The house may be unkempt or the children disorderly; there may not be peace, respect or honor shown in the family. There is not godliness or enjoyment there, and instead it is full of strife. People who live like this avoid having guests because they know that a house of feasting yet full of strife is worse than no feast, and no one wants to be there.[14]

Managing your home allows you to pursue hospitality. Have you ever considered that the condition of your home may be a hindrance to extending hospitality? I was recently reminded again of the priority of keeping my home orderly and well managed. My family and I were preparing to leave for a weekend trip to Grandma's house. As is my usual practice before leaving, I completed the general house cleaning, picked up the piles, and put the kids' toys away as a part of the trip preparations. We left our home on a Friday morning; two days later as we were about to return, my husband received a phone call from a friend letting us know that nine people had spent the night in our home the evening before!

A college missions team on a training exercise was looking for a place to stay and had showed up on our doorstep the night before. A friend with a key to our house was doing her laundry there when the team knocked at the door. She let the team in and agreed to stay with them for the night because, in her words, "She knew Mark and Lisa would not turn them away." While surprised by our unexpected guests in our absence, we were grateful that the Lord had used our home to provide a place of refuge for the students. Even though I was not expecting guests, I was not embarrassed by the condition of my home. I knew my home was generally clean and orderly. I try to live in anticipation of guests by, for example, keeping clean sheets on the guest bed.

Think for a moment how you would respond to unexpected guests. Would you be embarrassed by the condition of your home (dirty bathrooms, messy countertops, or unorganized piles of papers)? Managing your home allows you to practice hospitality with spontaneity and freedom. Try implementing the suggestions below for managing your home so that you are prepared to extend hospitality at any time.

Get organized. Choose one room to start with and then move through your home until each room is organized (this project may take you several weeks, but the results are worth it). What are you organizing? You are organizing the various parts of the room, including closets, cabinets, dresser drawers, and bookcases. Ideas for organizing include:

- creating storage space where needed;
- folding, straightening, or storing away clothes;
- cleaning out drawers and reorganizing cupboard space;
- throwing or giving away items not being used;
- filing paperwork.

Once your home is organized, it is much easier to keep it tidy and prepared because there is a place to put everything. You will no longer worry that a guest might open the "wrong" drawer or closet. After organizing the inside of your home, don't forget to organize the garage or other storage areas (attics, basements, or outside storage sheds). An organized home is one that is prepared to spontaneously welcome guests.

Establish a weekly cleaning schedule.[15] Cleaning is only difficult when it is not completed. Keeping up with the basic cleaning allows you to be prepared to receive unexpected guests at any time. Consistent cleaning makes planned events much easier also because you do not have to spend a lot of extra time trying to catch up with your cleaning before an event. Weekly cleaning in my home includes cleaning all bathrooms (tubs, toilets, sinks, and floors), polishing mirrors, vacuuming, dusting furniture, changing the bed linens, and mopping floors.

Identify daily cleaning chores. Completing a few simple cleaning tasks on a daily basis will make your weekly cleaning much easier. Also, it helps keep your home organized in between the major weekly cleanings. Daily tasks in my home include making beds, wiping countertops, sweeping the floor, emptying wastebaskets throughout the house, checking bathrooms (cleaning when needed—especially the toilets and sinks), picking up toys, and putting away the piles of paper, clothes, or other items that accumulate throughout the day. Take a few minutes every morning to complete your tasks or work on your list throughout the day. In my home, for example, I sweep daily after lunch and put away toys after dinner.

Problem solve for your organization challenges. You all have unique management challenges. Try to problem solve creatively for your family's organizational needs. For example, if you homeschool you will need to devise management strategies for storing schoolwork. A few of the problem areas I had to solve over the years include shoes, mail, books, and sunglasses. Below are some simple strategies that made a significant difference in the daily orderliness of my home:

- A basket for my children to put their shoes in (this has eliminated lost shoes as well as shoes lying around the house).
- A mail drawer for bills, paperwork to be filed, and other miscellaneous items related to school, church, or activities, which keeps the piles of paper out of sight.
- A notebook containing address lists and calendar dates for work, church, and school. It organizes in one location names, addresses, telephone numbers, e-mail ad-

dresses, and activity dates. We consult this notebook weekly.

- A small basket in the kitchen for my husband to store his keys, wallet, cell phone, and sunglasses.

All of these strategies are very simple; however, they have eliminated piles and facilitated organization in my home. I would encourage you to evaluate what needs to be addressed in your home.

Keep the pantry stocked. Extending hospitality usually involves food. Keeping your pantry stocked for a quick meal or snacks helps avoid last-minute trips to the grocery store. I usually keep frozen, ready-made raviolis and a jar of marinara sauce on hand. Also, I keep baking supplies for breads, desserts, or cookies. Finally, keep a supply of beverages (coffee, teas, soda, or juice). Keeping your pantry stocked reflects that you are living in anticipation of extending hospitality.

Prepare in advance for guests. Think about what "comfort" items you would like to have available for your guests. I keep clean sheets on our extra guest beds. I also have towels set aside as "guest" towels. By doing this I know they are ready and available for our guests. (They are also kept in better condition because my family is not using them on a daily basis). Other items to keep on hand for guests to use and enjoy include magazines, music CDs, novels, snacks, and extra toiletry items such as shampoo or toothbrushes. Even if you do not have a designated guest room, you can still plan ahead in anticipation of how you will provide for your guests. For example, purchase sleeping bags so your children can sleep on the floor or an air mattress to provide an extra bed.

Straighten up before going to bed. Take five minutes to walk around the house and make sure everything is generally picked up. Straighten the couch pillows, throw away old newspapers, put away toys, start the dishwasher, or pick up the projects you have been working on (crafts, paperwork, etc.).

Understand that orderliness, not perfection, is your goal. Managing your home in anticipation of extending hospitality is only one of your priorities. Preparation for guests should never alienate your own family members by creating a sterile, untouchable home. Your home is first for your family. As we discussed in chapter 3, keeping an orderly home is for their benefit as well. Maintaining an orderly home does not mean you do not live in your home—your husband will still have his piles of newspaper, your children will have toys throughout the house, and you may have a craft project in process. Organization simply means you have a system for maintaining a basic level of cleanliness and organization. There will still be times when guests arrive and the floor needs to be swept, or there are piles of paper on the counter; that is part of welcoming guests into your family as well as your home. Your goal is simply to make cleaning and organizing a regular habit so that you experience greater freedom in opening your home.

Have a proper perspective on possessions. The purpose of organization is to prepare your home and possessions to be *used* and enjoyed by your guests—not to preserve them. Just as organization should not alienate the people in your home, it should also not limit the use of your possessions or home. This means that things will wear out, break, and look worn at times. Joann Cairns provides a good reminder of the attitude we should have toward using our possessions when practicing hospitality. She says this about the use of her guest room:

> The furnishings of your home will wear out more rapidly when you practice hospitality. The nightstand will inevitably develop a telltale ring from the wet glass a guest places on the bare wood. The bedspreads and carpets begin to show worn spots. Dishes are broken and appliances whine and hesitate when they used to hum. Now, an unused guest room could

last a lifetime and still look like new, but then it wouldn't really be a guest room, would it?[16]

Prepare for Graciousness

"A gracious woman gets honor" (Prov. 11:16). While most desire to embrace the biblical mandate for extending hospitality, many of you do not practice hospitality with ease and enjoyment. There are a variety of reasons why, but often merely a lack of experience combined with a lack of adequate planning robs you of joy and graciousness. What does it mean to be a gracious woman in the context of hospitality?

Gracious means you are kind, courteous, and cordial.[17] In the context of hospitality, *graciousness* is evident in how our guests are greeted and then treated while in our home. A hostess should desire to respond in graciousness at all times—regardless of the behavior of her guests (late arrival, poor table etiquette, or lack of gratitude) and circumstances (appliance failure, burnt food, or misbehaving children). Although there will always be uncontrollable circumstances, management allows you to prepare in advance as much as possible. Your graciousness can be threatened when you have not planned appropriately and organized the details of the event. Management, therefore, becomes a tool you can use to help facilitate a gracious environment for your guests.

There are many practical steps that can help you be successful when practicing hospitality. I have found that when I give thought to the following areas I am better prepared to enjoy the event and respond to my guests with graciousness.

Develop Reliable Menus[18]

Most of the work related to practicing hospitality revolves around the preparation of the food. There are other areas to manage such as cleaning the house, but most of the unique tasks for entertaining are centered around the planning of, shopping for, and preparation of the food. Developing your menu is the first key to successful hospitality. A menu simply lists the food you will be preparing and serving for each entertainment opportunity. Selecting the appropriate menu is a key to your success as a hostess. Following are several things to remember when planning your menus.

Plan easy menus until you develop your hostess skills. Once you begin to exercise hospitality on a regular basis, you will be able to expand the type of menus you prepare. Plan menus that coincide with your experience. (If you have no experience, ask your mother or a friend for recipes that have proven to be easy.)

Plan menus that complement your time limitations. You may have the ability to prepare a delicious gourmet dinner, but your availability may limit what you can successfully prepare without stress. For example, mothers with young children often do not entertain because they feel they have no time, when in reality if they selected simple menus with items that could be prepared ahead of time, they would be able to entertain regularly—even with small children in the house.

Develop menus that are appropriate for the group size. I usually determine this by the amount of time it takes to prepare the main course; if a menu is time consuming, I reserve it for use with smaller groups. Here are two examples:

SIMPLE MENU FOR A LARGE GROUP
Spaghetti with Marinara Sauce
Garden Salad
Italian Herb Bread (use bread machine)
Chocolate Chip Bundt Cake

INTERMEDIATE MENU FOR A SMALL GROUP

Chicken Manicotti with Roasted Vegetables
Mashed Garlic Potatoes
Candied Pecan and Pear Salad
Pumpkin Cheesecake

Some of the menu items for the large group (spaghetti sauce, bread, and dessert) can be prepared in advance; in contrast to this, the intermediate menu reflects items that cannot be prepared in advance (with the exception of the cheesecake, which can be prepared one day in advance). The second menu is also difficult to prepare for a large group because it is not cost effective (too much variety in the ingredients).

Collect recipes that can be made ahead of time. This allows you to be able to work ahead during the week and makes the actual entertainment date less hectic. While you might not be able to prepare the whole menu in advance, usually you can plan menus that have parts already prepared. For example, many entrees, breads, or desserts can be prepared in advance and frozen.

Develop a Family Favorites recipe file. This file box (mine is a small recipe notebook) contains all the recipes your family enjoys most. It can save you a lot of time when you are planning menus. Instead of thumbing through various cookbooks, you simply grab your Family Favorites file, and you have the recipes all in one location. You know how to fix these recipes, and you know they taste good. I also keep all of my mom's recipes that have been handed down to me in my Family Favorites files. I have a second file box for general recipes; a recipe does not go into the Family Favorites file until it has been used several times.

Save your menu plans. Keep a record of the menus you prepare—you will eventually be able to reuse them. Be sure to note the cookbook name and page number on the menu if you do not include the recipe so that you will be able to locate it in the future.

Set up a Hospitality Notebook.[19] This is a useful resource to help you organize any entertaining event. You can modify the sections of the notebook to meet your specific entertainment needs. Below are some suggestions to get you started.

- Section One: Event Preparations—a place to identify event purpose and theme.
- Section Two: Guest Information—a place for information related to your guests and their specific needs (names, addresses, phone numbers, e-mail addresses, diet restrictions, and RSVP information).
- Section Three: Ideas—this is the place to keep ideas for new recipes or decorating ideas you would like to try.
- Section Four: Resources—a place to keep contact information for entertainment service providers (florists, caterers, rental companies, party stores, pizza delivery, and specialty stores).
- Section Five: Menu Planning—a place to store written menus for each event so that you can locate them easily the next time you desire to use them. Also, you can create an actual timetable for the menu items you select. Indicate time for pre-preparation, cooking, and serving for each item. The timetable allows you to identify when you need to begin preparing each item; it is the key to having everything ready at the same time.
- Section Six: Evaluation and Memorable Moments—a place to record notes to help you improve your hosting and entertaining skills. If you do not take the time to identify what you have learned from your experiences, you will continue to make the same mistakes. Also, we often forget to record the blessings of hospitality; it is

important to take time to reflect on the most enjoyable or challenging moments.

Plan menus that reflect a variety of food types, tastes, and textures. I try to have something from every food group in the food pyramid (meats/fish, dairy/cheese, breads/cereals/pastas, fruits, and vegetables). If each food group is represented, you are quite sure to have a tasty, well-planned menu.

Collect Practical Linens and Table Decorations

When you first begin to entertain, you usually are limited in the amount of money that you can spend on linens and table decorations. It might take some time to build up your supplies, but if you make careful selections you will be able to service most occasions with a minimal amount of linens and decorations. A few guidelines to maximize your resources include the following:

- Begin with basic colors for table linens. Purchase white, cream, or other neutral colors such as tan or, if you are a bride to be, include basic colors from your bridal registry. A neutral tablecloth can be used for all occasions and seasons. If your resources are limited, wait to purchase specialty colors.
- Plan ahead so that you can take time to carefully collect functional linens that can be used for a variety of occasions. Only purchase linens when they are on sale.
- Add variety to your basic table linens by collecting seasonal napkins; for example, if you have a cream tablecloth, you can add napkins in the seasonal orange and brown colors at Thanksgiving or green and burgundy at Christmas. Remember to purchase the seasonal items on clearance after the holiday.
- Create a seasonal decoration box. I keep a seasonal decoration box in our garage. It is full of items that I can

reuse for table decorations. Some of the generic items in my box include silk sunflowers, strands of ivy, small American flags, and strings of wooden red beads. Other items are related to specific occasions such as small wooden Pilgrim people and baby blocks. All are items that can be used for various holidays or celebrations such as baby showers, bridal showers, or teas. Keeping a box of reusable items saves both time and money for most entertainment events. As with the table linens, purchase these items on clearance after the season is over and you will have them to use the following year.

- Decorate with candles, candles, and more candles! Candles work for almost any celebration or holiday. Collecting a few simple candle holders will allow you to create a warm ambience for any occasion. Be creative in your display by varying the size, shape, and height; they do not all have to match.

Establish a Purpose for Your Hospitality

Oftentimes you do not practice hospitality simply because you do not take the time to *plan intentionally* to extend hospitality. Your calendars are full, the days slip away into weeks, and before you know it another month has passed without inviting people into your home. A crucial part of successful hospitality is to be *purpose-driven*. You sit down (with your spouse if you are married) and determine in advance those to whom you would like to extend hospitality. Consider making a list of individuals you would like to entertain and a brief statement of your goals for each event. When your list is complete you can review your calendar and begin to select entertainment dates. The goal or purpose for the event will help to guide your conversation and influence how you will order the event's activities. Your hospitality list might look something like this:

TABLE 4.1

Sample Hospitality Purpose Sheet

Guests	Purpose
Pastor and wife	Communicate gratitude for their ministry; be an encouragement to them as a couple
International students	Learn about their culture, and a witnessing opportunity (outreach from our home)
Family	Grow relationships, communicate love, and celebrate family events
Neighbors	Gospel witness and establishing relationships

Remember, however, the hospitality list is not intended to preempt spontaneity; rather, it is designed to help facilitate hospitality and bring meaning to the events you are planning. It is just a tool to help prevent your busy schedules from thwarting your attempts to exercise hospitality. It can also help remind you how to pray before each event.

Plan for the Unexpected

Regardless of how well you have planned, there will always be unexpected and uncontrollable events. Some examples I have experienced include late guests, those who did not RSVP to an event, unexpected guests, guests calling at the moment they should be arriving to say they are not coming, desserts that failed on the day of the event, meat that did not cook on time, broken appliances, leaving the burner on high too long and having burnt food, power failure, sick children, and other health issues like getting a migraine headache. The list could go on and on! Most of life is not controllable. Therefore, it is important to remember one principle: "A gracious woman gets honor" (Prov. 11:16). Your primary goal in all hospitality opportunities is to maintain a gracious spirit. While you cannot plan for every uncontrollable circumstance, you can be prepared for several unexpected events in the following ways.

Pray, pray, pray (1 Thess. 5:16–18)! Always take the time to pray before an event. Through the Lord's strength you are able to maintain a gracious spirit in the midst of uncontrollable circumstances. If you take time to commit the event to the Lord, you relinquish control of the event to him. Therefore, whatever happens—good or bad—you can rest quietly and confidently knowing that the Lord is working out his sovereign will. By taking the time to pray you are more likely to maintain a calm spirit rather than trying to fix everything in your own strength.

Complete as much work as possible in advance. Start a week before your event and accomplish tasks that can be done ahead—grocery shopping, preparing and freezing a dessert, or cleaning the house. This advance work allows you time to handle the unexpected.

Prepare extra food. By preparing extra food you will be able to graciously receive those guests who did not RSVP or who RSVPed late. I would suggest that, rather than risking offending your guests or damaging a relationship, you simply prepare enough food for all the guests you invite. This allows you to respond with graciousness any time. It also saves time and energy by preventing additional trips to the grocery store. If you have leftover food, your family can enjoy it the following day, or send the leftovers home with your guests. I have rarely wasted the extra food!

Keep basic supplies on hand. You will always have unexpected guests; by keeping basic supplies on hand you will be able to prepare a meal, snack, or dessert quickly. I try to keep supplies on hand for a complete meal, and I always have the ingredients to make chocolate chip or oatmeal cookies. The supplies you store will vary according to the recipes you select. I have found over the years it is helpful to keep the following supplies in the cupboard or refrigerator:

- baking supplies (flour, sugars—white, brown, and powdered—baking soda, baking powder, vanilla, and yeast) for biscuits, pie crusts, cookies, or quick breads;

- biscuit mix (I make one from scratch, but you can also buy ready-made) for waffles, pancakes, and quick breads;
- chocolate chips for cookies, icing, and garnishes;
- dried cranberries or raisins for scones and coffee cakes;
- walnuts or pecans for salads, poultry dishes, cookies, and garnishes;
- buttermilk for scones, banana muffins, and pancakes;
- cake, brownie, and cornbread ready-made mixes;
- pasta (various types of noodles such as spaghetti, wagon wheels, or lasagna) with ready-made tomato or Alfredo sauces for quick dinners;
- grated cheese for pizza, tacos, lasagna (cheese can be frozen to prevent spoiling);
- canned or frozen vegetables (green beans, corn, or peas);
- special bread machine supplies (several recipes for my bread machine require dry powdered milk, honey, or lemon juice);
- canned goods—soups, tomato sauce (for marinara sauces), black olives (for breads, sauces, or quesadillas), and mandarin oranges (for salads).

Encourage Meaningful Conversation

As the hostess we should be prepared to stimulate thoughtful conversation that is both edifying and encouraging to our guests. It took me several years of entertaining to truly grasp the importance of planning for the conversation. I can remember many events when I did not pray prior to the event or ask thoughtful questions of my guests, and unfortunately I was always disappointed at the end of the event. The food may have been perfectly prepared, the house was clean, the guests arrived on time, and other details fell into place flawlessly, but the occasion was still a disappointment.

Why? Because we spent the time on worthless chitchat. The guests came and went without really getting to know each other better or meeting a specific need.

How disappointing! Planning meaningful conversation will help you be more effective in your ability to meet the needs of your guests. Additionally, planning conversation helps guests feel more at ease by preventing long periods of silence. A wise hostess will be intentional in guiding the conversation by praying about the conversation before the event begins. Pray that the conversation will be edifying (Rom. 15:1–2) and encouraging (1 Thess. 5:11) to your guests.

A wise hostess will be intentional in identifying the needs of her guests. Whatever needs are represented by our guests, we should endeavor to meet them. Do they need spiritual encouragement? Physical rest? Confrontation about sin issues? Our counsel? Simply someone to listen?

A wise hostess will be intentional in soliciting the counsel and advice of her guests. Every guest in our home represents a unique set of life circumstances. If they are believers, God is also completing a unique work in their lives. We often neglect to take advantage of the wisdom represented in our guests. By asking intentional questions we reflect a humble and teachable spirit. Questions you might consider are:

- How did they raise their godly children?
- How do they keep their marriage strong?
- Have they traveled to countries you desire to visit? Can you learn from their ministry experiences?

A wise hostess will be intentional in thinking in advance of questions she can ask her guests. My husband and I have generated a list of questions that helps guide our conversations. We do not ask every question, but our list does help us make the most of the time with our guests.

- When and how did they come to know the Lord (their Christian testimony)?
- What are their family backgrounds (where were they raised, how many siblings do they have, etc.)?
- What has been their church involvement or ministry experience?
- What are some of their family traditions?
- How do they celebrate holidays?
- What are their hobbies or what do they do during their free time?
- Where have they traveled and why were they there?
- Do they have any needs we can help them with, or how can we pray specifically for them?
- What is the Lord teaching them during this period of their lives?
- What advice can they give to us (the topics are chosen based on the individual life experiences and ages of our guests, such as parenting or marriage).
- What long-term goals do they have (for example, what would they like to be doing five, ten, or twenty years from now)?

There are many areas to organize, plan, and prepare when entertaining guests in your home. By investing the time and energy to think in advance about your menus, supplies, and goals for hospitality, you will be free to focus on what is most important in biblical hospitality—people—and meeting their needs.

A Concluding Consideration

Developing good management strategies will help you maximize your time, energy, and resources. However, it is easy in the context of discussing management to forget *why* you are managing. Remember the purpose of hospitality is to model God's love to people. Believers are motivated to love others because God first loved them (1 John 4:19). Management is merely a tool in the process of practicing hospitality. Doris Greig, author of *We Didn't Know They Were Angels*, suggests that your attitude toward extending hospitality should be *relaxed availability*. Her words are a fitting reminder to the proper attitude we should have while implementing management strategies:

> We need to remember to pray and invite the Lord to be our guide and guest whenever we open our hearts and homes. In this way, the Holy Spirit will be in charge of our hospitality and it will be warm and relaxed because of the Lord. Whether we have guests for 15 minutes, an evening, overnight, or for a matter of weeks, we need to ask Christ to bring His peace into our household so that it will be evident to all. May it be our goal, as well as our prayer, to be relaxed, available, and good listeners. If so, He will enable us to enjoy our guests. They in turn will know God's blessing through our relaxed, available hospitality, whatever the occasion or length of time.[20]

May you always remember that management is merely a tool used to prepare your home for the purpose of extending hospitality to those the Lord brings into your life.

Practicing Hospitality

1. Review what Scripture has to say about idleness and diligence. Complete the following chart and then add to the list by doing additional study. Once you have completed your study, pray and ask the Lord to help you identify areas where you are idle, and pray for wisdom to make the necessary changes in your habits.

Topic	Summary of Principles	Application
Idleness		The consequences of idleness are:
Proverbs 13:4		
Proverbs 18:9		
Proverbs 19:15		
Proverbs 20:4, 13		
Proverbs 21:25		
Proverbs 24:30–31, 34		
Proverbs 26:15–16		
Romans 12:11		
Hebrews 6:12		
Diligence		Areas in which I need to make changes to practice diligence in my life and home are:
Proverbs 6:6–11		
Proverbs 10:4		
Proverbs 12:24, 27		
Proverbs 30:25–26		
Proverbs 31:27		
1 Thessalonians 5:14		
2 Thessalonians 3:6		
1 Timothy 5:13		

2. Are you a planner for generosity? Consider what practical steps you need to complete in order to be prepared to extend hospitality. Begin by evaluating the following areas:

- Do you need to stock your pantry? If so, make a shopping list and purchase the needed supplies.
- Do you know of a person in need? If so, call to make arrangements to deliver a meal or ask how you can serve him.
- Does your church have missionaries visiting in the near future? If so, volunteer to have them stay in your home or to come for lunch after church.
- Are your children involved in church activities? If so, volunteer your home for a meeting location for Bible studies or other events.

3. Do you need to organize or clean your home so you are prepared to extend hospitality? Walk through your home, room by room. Identify areas that need to be organized

or cleaned. Also, make a list of supplies you will need to facilitate organization such as storage containers. Use the chart below to help you identify the needs of your home. Modify it to reflect the specific rooms in your house. Once you have identified your needs, establish a plan for organizing each room.

Location	Organizing Needs	Supplies Needed
Living room/family room		
Dining room		
Kitchen		
Master bedroom		
Children's rooms		
Guest room/office		
Laundry/linen closets		
Garage/storage areas		

4. Set up your Hospitality Notebook. Begin by using the sections suggested in this chapter; modify the notebook to meet your personal needs.

5. Proverbs 11:16 states, "A gracious woman gets honor." Are you a gracious woman? What threatens your graciousness when extending hospitality? Review the Scripture below. Identify how graciousness is manifested in your speech, thoughts, and actions. Pray and ask the Lord to mature you into a gracious woman, regardless of the behavior of your guests or the circumstances of your life.

Am I Gracious In:	
My Thoughts?	Romans 12:2; 2 Corinthians 10:3–5; Philippians 4:8–9
My Speech?	Matthew 12:33–37; Ephesians 4:25–32; Colossians 4:6
My Actions?	Galatians 5:13–25; Philippians 2:3–7; Titus 3:1–7

Recipe Resources

The chapter focused on implementing effective management strategies. Hospitality events usually involve preparing food. The four strategies given below may be helpful in managing your food preparation. A sample recipe is given for each suggestion:

- Use recipes that can be prepared in advance and frozen (Baked Spaghetti).
- Use simple and quick recipes (Pasta Fagioli Soup).
- Use appliances to lighten the work load such as a bread machine or Crock-Pot (Italian Herb Bread).
- Use ready-made or partially made items (Homemade Biscuit Mix).

Baked Spaghetti

1 cup chopped onion
1 cup chopped green pepper
1 tablespoon butter
1 can (28-ounce) tomatoes, cut, with liquid
1 can (4-ounce) mushroom pieces
1 can (2¼-ounce) sliced olives
2 tablespoons oregano
1 pound ground beef, cooked and drained
12 ounces spaghetti, cooked and drained
2 cups (8 ounces) shredded cheddar cheese
1 can (10¾-ounce) cream of mushroom soup
¼ cup water
¼ cup Parmesan cheese

In a large skillet, sauté onion and green pepper in butter until tender. Add tomatoes, mushrooms, olives, oregano, and ground beef. Simmer, uncovered, 10 minutes. Place half the spaghetti in a greased 13 x 9 x 2 baking dish. Top with half the vegetable/meat mixture. Sprinkle with 1 cup of the cheddar cheese. Repeat layers.

Mix soup and water. Pour over top of casserole. Sprinkle with Parmesan cheese. Bake uncovered at 350 degrees for 30–35 minutes or until heated through.

Serves about 12

Pasta Fagioli Soup

1 pound 95% lean ground beef
1 teaspoon crushed garlic
1 medium-size onion, chopped
1 large carrot, peeled, halved, sliced
2 large stalks celery, chopped
2 cans (14 ounces each) crushed tomatoes
1 tablespoon beef bouillon granules
2½ teaspoons dried Italian seasonings
¼ teaspoon pepper
4 cups water
1 can (1 lb.) kidney beans, drained
6 ounces pasta (2¼ cups) (ziti or wagon wheels)

Spray pan with nonstick spray. Add ground beef and garlic. Crumble and cook until no pink remains. Drain off excess fat. Add remaining ingredients except beans and pasta. Bring to a boil; reduce heat and simmer about 15 minutes or until vegetables are tender. Add beans and pasta; bring to a boil. Reduce heat and simmer 9 minutes or until pasta is cooked (don't overcook, as pasta keeps cooking in hot soup).

Serves about 12

Italian Herb Bread
(for bread machine)

For 1 pound:
¾ cup water
1 tablespoon olive oil
1 teaspoon lemon juice
1 teaspoon salt
1 tablespoon sugar
1 tablespoon dried milk
2 cups bread flour
2 teaspoons Italian seasoning
1 teaspoon active dry yeast

For 1½ pounds:
¾ cup plus 2 tablespoons water
2 tablespoons olive oil
1 teaspoon lemon juice
1 teaspoon salt
2 tablespoons sugar
2 tablespoons dried milk
3 cups bread flour
1 tablespoon Italian seasoning
1 teaspoon active dry yeast

Place ingredients in bread pan in the order listed. Press the SELECT pad until FRENCH BAKE appears in the display window. (Tip: yeast amounts are correct. Delay cycle is not recommended.) Bread will be completed in 3 hours and 43 minutes. Remove bread pan from the bread box. Invert and shake to remove loaf. Cool on wire rack.

Homemade Biscuit Mix

3 cups flour
½ cup nonfat dry powdered milk

2 tablespoons baking powder
¾ teaspoon salt
⅓ cup canola or corn oil

Mix the dry ingredients. Slowly pour the oil into the mixture and blend well using either electric mixer or pastry blender. Store in a cool place in a covered container.

Makes about 3 loosely packed cups

Low-fat Biscuits

1½ cups biscuit mix
⅓ cup skim milk

Heat oven to 450 degrees. Mix ingredients. Flatten dough until it is ½-inch thick and then cut. Bake 8–10 minutes.

Makes 8 biscuits

Buttermilk Biscuits

2 cups biscuit mix
⅔ cup buttermilk
¼ teaspoon baking soda

Heat oven to 450 degrees. Mix all ingredients. Flatten dough until it is ½-inch thick and then cut. Bake 8–10 minutes.

Makes 12 biscuits

5

Hospitality and YOUR HOME

Beloved, I urge you as sojourners and exiles to abstain from the passions of the flesh, which wage war against your soul. Keep your conduct among the Gentiles honorable, so that when they speak against you as evildoers, they may see your good deeds and glorify God on the day of visitation.

—1 PETER 2:11–12

What is a home? To the architect it is an amalgamation of design features. To the contractor it is the assembly of an assortment of building materials, while to the interior designer it is a backdrop for the aesthetic application of color, texture, fabrics, and accessories. A home from a biblical perspective, however, is to be a place of *refuge* and a center for *evangelism*.

131

The Home as a Place of Refuge

"He who dwells in the shelter of the Most High will abide in the shadow of the Almighty. I will say to the LORD, 'My refuge and my fortress, my God, in whom I trust'" (Ps. 91:1–2). *Refuge*, by definition, means a "shelter or protection from danger, trouble, etc.; anything to which one has recourse for aid, relief or escape."[1] Scripture is filled with illustrations of refuges provided by God. The illustrations describe qualities that are to be characteristic of the Christian home, first to those who reside there and then to those who are welcomed as a gesture of biblical hospitality. According to Scripture the Christian home is to be a place of:

- refuge for those who have done wrong (Num. 35:6, 11–15);
- safety (Num. 35:25–28);
- protection that mirrors the illustration of God providing shelter as a mother bird shelters the young and fragile with her wings (Ex.19:4; Deut. 32:11; Ps. 17:8; 36:7; 57:1; 61:4; 63:7; 91:1–4);
- security—a stronghold that is safe from the hostility of the world (2 Sam. 22:3);[2]
- refreshment for those who communicate the gospel (Luke 10:38–42; Acts 9:35–10:23; 16:15; Rom. 12:13; 16:23; Heb. 13:2; 1 Pet. 4:9; Philem. 22; 3 John 5–8).

Our homes become places of *refuge* for others as we choose to use our hospitality skills to minister to them. A myriad of opportunities exist. Let's explore some that were shared by trained women who responded to our survey, women who have practiced hospitality.[3]

Melitsa Barnes offers to provide snacks or meals for special church events or Bible studies and is willing to teach other women what it means to be hospitable.

Lisa-Ann Chun invites girls for discipleship and light refreshments and also welcomes people into her home for dinner, fellowship, and evangelism.

Missionaries to Mexico, Luis and Robin Contreras, host monthly church leadership meetings in their home. Robin provides light refreshments, greets the guests when they arrive, and bids them farewell as they leave. Their home is always available for people who might want to visit or come by.

Lisa DiGiacomo writes that one thing her husband taught her is that she does not need to leave her front door to be ministering. As she prepares a nice meal for her family and makes home a haven, she is truly ministering to them. Beyond these daily kinds of ministries, the DiGiacomos see every guest—expected or not—in their home as someone they have the opportunity to care for. A friend dropping by unannounced or guests invited for supper or a holiday all provide opportunities for their family to give of themselves. Lisa enjoys having college-aged girls over for coffee while her own girls are napping. She also opens their home for Bible studies.

As the wife of a pastor, practicing hospitality is a regular part of Sue Edwards's ministry. Whether it is providing shelter, sanctuary, meals, a cup of water, or a listening ear, their home is always open to those who need them, their time, or their possessions.

Vicki Ferretti says that because her husband, Bryan, is in ministry full time, they regularly hold high school staff meetings in their home, which has been a hangout for youth groups and for events throughout their marriage and ministry together. A missionary-in-training and a pastor who spoke at a men's conference held at their church also have stayed with them.

Kelli Gleeson and her husband consider it a privilege to welcome people to their home. Once a month they host a meeting for all the Sunday school team leaders (about fifteen people). She serves a nice lunch and dessert. They also try to have a family or a couple over twice a month, just to get to know them and to bless them with Christ's love. The Gleesons' philosophy is, "It is our desire that those who enter our home will sense something different, a sense of love, peace and warmth. A Christian home should be a safe haven or refuge from the world outside. We pray that our lives are a testimony of God's grace and his goodness. As people who come to our home get to know us, we pray that they will see a difference in our marriage and the way that we live our daily lives."

Anne Johnson and her husband are on high school staff at their church. She focuses on imparting skills to her small group of girls when she invites them to their apartment.

Connie Naresh weekly uses hospitality skills in ministry. For several years she and her husband held a college Bible study in their home; they wanted the students who attended to feel welcome and accepted. Now, at different seasons of the year, they invite others into their home for fellowship and fun, and they seek to make their apartment available for a night's lodging to people traveling through their area.

Dave and Peggy Rowan's home is a place of refuge in a variety of ways: missionaries, needy and troubled people such as children with unfit parents, single people, pregnant women, homeless, and emotionally troubled youth have stayed overnight and shared meals. They have hosted meals for college students and had college students live with them in the summer. Peggy shares honestly:

> You know, Dr. Ennis, that I wasn't a prize pupil in home economics, and sometimes I am embarrassed, not because I chose the major, but because I don't want the major to look bad because of me! But I did learn some things at college.

I didn't know how to cook at all when I came to Christian Heritage College, so living in the Home Management house helped me. I remember taking Meal Management. When the professor discussed etiquette, she said most of the content was probably review. Well, a lot of it was new to me! I didn't have a rude family, but we were pretty basic: "fork on the left, knife and spoon on the right, and pass the food instead of reaching." Now I was learning about all these different kinds of plates, silverware, and glassware and the placement of these things—yikes! But the greatest thing she said was that proper etiquette isn't as important as making people feel comfortable.

The best thing about home economics was that it helped me gain a biblical perspective on hospitality. I learned that the Bible teaches me about serving others; submitting to my husband (even when I think he invites people over too much or doesn't spend enough money on the house!); humility (when I think I'm not good enough or my things aren't nice enough); being a good steward; trusting God for provisions and safety (some people we've had in our home scared me); and remembering that giving a cup of cold water in the name of Jesus is doing it unto him.[4]

Peggy's vulnerable conclusions remind us that as we allow our homes to be a refuge for others, we will be fulfilling the instruction recorded in 1 Peter 2:11–12.

The Home as a Center for Evangelism

"They are to do good, to be rich in good works, to be generous and ready to share" (1 Tim. 6:18). The church of the twenty-first century has cultivated highly sophisticated procedures and tools for evangelism—training sessions, videos, seminars, manuals, and methodology books are all available. However, as you study Scripture you find that the home, not the church, served as the center for evangelism in the early expansion of Christianity. Michael Green writes, "One of the most important methods of spreading the gospel in antiquity was the use of homes."[5] He then affirms the home of Aquila and Priscilla by stating, "Homes like this must have been exceedingly effective in the evangelistic outreach of the church."[6]

Vonette Bright, who along with her husband, Bill, founded Campus Crusade for Christ in 1951, encourages Christian women to use their homes as a center for evangelism. Writing in *The Joy of Hospitality* she explains how hospitality can build bridges to those who need Christ:

> Hospitality is more than entertaining. It is expecting God to do great things through you as you reach out to touch the lives of others. It is focusing our relationships, especially the greatest relationship of all—walking and talking with the Lord Jesus Christ. True hospitality doesn't wear us out or make us feel pressured; life-sharing is not entertaining in our own strength. It flows from a heart full of love for others. Christ's love, which doesn't come from our self-effort, is a work of the Holy Spirit in our lives. The love of Christ is what draws people to God. This love transforms a party or other event into true hospitality. Hospitality, then, is not an event; it is genuine concern for another's well-being.[7]

An excursion through New Testament Scriptures gives us insight into the importance of practicing evangelism. Our Lord's final instruction to his disciples was to make disciples, not merely converts, of all nations (Matt. 28:19).

Also, Paul writes that our Lord gave spiritual gifts, including the gift of *evangelist*, to those he called into service (Eph. 4:11). Repeating the term in 2 Timothy 4:5, Paul directs believers to "do the work of an *evangelist*." John MacArthur provides insight on this passage by defining *evangelist* for us:

> Used only two other times in the [New Testament] (Acts 21:8; Eph. 4:1), this word always refers to a specific office of ministry for the purpose of preaching the gospel to non-Christians. Based on Eph. 4:11, it is very basic to assume that all churches would have both pastor-teachers and evangelists.

But the related verb "to preach the gospel" and the related noun "gospel" are used throughout the [New Testament] not only in relation to evangelists, but also to the call for every Christian, especially preachers and teachers, to proclaim the gospel. Paul did not call Timothy to the office of an evangelist, but to "do the work" of one.[8]

As with the concept of our homes becoming places of refuge for others, they become *centers for evangelism* when they are dedicated to our Lord; unlimited opportunities exist as our survey respondents indicated:[9]

- Bonnie Bishop recently purchased her first home, which expanded her opportunity for hospitality. Her first experience was hosting a Bible study social not quite one week after moving in. The décor was more stacked boxes than anything else, but the evening was definitely a success.
- A pastor's wife, Becky Ellsworth, invites unchurched neighbors for dessert, and her children bring home their public-school friends. She candidly says, "I can't say that we often sit down and share the gospel, but our lives are centered on Christ and we don't hide that."
- Elizabeth Gilbert invited several members of her sons' chess club to their home for a fun tournament and a cookout. Gary cooked up the hamburgers and developed a nice tract for chess players, which was given to each one before they left the event. She seeks to have a good supply of tracts available for anyone who comes to her door.
- Taking advantage of the Christmas season, Tracie Priske invites friends and neighbors to her home to bake and to address Christmas cards. It's a fun way to fellowship and share Christ with others!
- Jason and Heather Lanker invite their unsaved neighbors over for dinner about once every two weeks. The conversation is sometimes geared towards Christianity,

and they have the opportunity to share their faith with them. Also, people who are selling things door-to-door are sometimes invited for dinner—they come too! The guests ask questions, and naturally they ask about Jason's profession; he tells them he's a pastor and that leads to many discussions.

- J. J. and Maria VanderJagt share Christ with others in their home by creating an atmosphere that is calm and peaceful, not one filled with chaos and restlessness. They believe that letting people know that their home is available gives them a sense of comfort and ease so that Christ can be shared. Finally, just by having their home open to different church activities is a way to witness to their neighbors. Neighbors see the cars parked and at times may hear some conversations about God when the guests are talking outside, and they most likely can hear the singing.

- Believing she can share Christ with others only as she has them in her home and gives of her emotions, time, and resources to minister, Patti Morse writes, "Truly, people do not care what you know until they know how much you care. Our greatest commodity in this world is our time, and our greatest possessions are those we have in our home. To share both with a heart of love and compassion is the ultimate springboard for sharing the greatest gift of all . . . Jesus Christ!" She suggests that this can be done through dinner fellowships, luncheons, teas, craft parties, children's events, coffee chats, holiday fests, open houses, and walking with partners. The necessary ingredient is a selfless, loving heart in which the love of God has been shed abroad (Rom. 5:5) and in which a burden for the lost has been placed.

Let's develop one of Patti's suggestions, a tea, and at the same time focus on consecrating our china for our Master's use.

Consecrating Our China for Our Master's Use

"He who offered his offering the first day was Nahshon the son of Amminadab, of the tribe of Judah. And his offering was one silver plate whose weight was 130 shekels, one silver basin of 70 shekels, according to the shekel of the sanctuary, both of them full of fine flour mixed with oil for a grain offering" (Num. 7:12–13). As you approach this section of this chapter, "Hospitality and Your Home," an initial response could be, "This section does not apply to me—I do not have china." That may be true, but you do have vessels in which you serve food. These vessels may be bone china, stoneware, carthenware, plastic, stainless steel, pewter, enamelware, silver, wood, or paper. The material from which our vessels are made is not the question; the question is, have the vessels been consecrated to our Master's use?

Consecration, by definition, is the action of making or declaring sacred, dedicating to the service of a deity, devoting or dedicating to some service, or hallowing.[10] As you consider consecrating your vessels to the heavenly Father, you must first acknowledge the most significant consecration as believers—the consecration of yourself! When your life is consecrated to him, you are able to acknowledge that you are unable to practice biblical hospitality without his blessing; you will acknowledge that you are like the vessel Paul describes in 2 Corinthians 4:7—lowly, common, expendable, and replaceable.

However, because you belong to the heavenly Father, his power overcomes your weaknesses and allows you to be a vessel used for his honor and glory (2 Cor. 12:9–10). Frances Havergal summarizes this thought by writing, "Full consecration may be in one sense the act of a moment and in another the work of a lifetime. It must be complete to be real, and yet—if real it is always incomplete. Consecration is a point of rest and yet a perpetual progression."[11] Once salvation, "the act of a moment," is completed, you are then ready for the "perpetual progression." As a part of your perpetual progression, let's examine some *tea tips* that make use of your consecrated china to implement one of Patti Morse's suggestions.

Hostessing a Consecrated China Tea

"Oh, taste and see that the LORD is good! Blessed is the man who takes refuge in him!" (Ps. 34:8). Shortly after the release of *If Tea Cups Could Talk*, one of the first Christian books that communicated the importance of taking time to share a cup of tea with friends and family, a Victorian tearoom opened in my community. Since it was close to Lisa's birthday, I asked her if she would enjoy celebrating her birthday over tea; her response was affirmative so I made a reservation for us. Housed in the rear of an upscale boutique, the tearoom was separated from the shop by a lovely lace curtain. As the time of our reservation approached we were seated, the lace curtain was released from its ornate brackets, and a gracious ambience surrounded us that prompted a time of warmth, sharing, and celebration.

Emilie Barnes captures the essence of our first tea experience as she writes, "It's not the tea that makes teatime special, it's the spirit of the tea party. It's what happens when women or men or children make a place in their life for the rituals of sharing. It's what happens when we bother with the little extras that feed the soul and nurture the senses and make space for unhurried conversation. And when that happens, it doesn't really matter what fills the cups or holds the liquid."[12] Since the celebration of Lisa's birthday we have chosen to "do tea" on a number of occasions, and each time created another link in our friendship chain.

Whether you are planning an intimate tea for two, an elaborate Victorian tea, or packing up your vessels in a basket to serve tea in a location other than your home, ponder the

Teatime Tips that follow and then implement the ones that will help you create links in your friendship chains.

Teatime Tips

"Come and share a pot of tea, my home is warm and my friendship's free."[13] Begin your planning time with a *prayer of consecration*. It is helpful to write out the prayer, review it each time you entertain, and modify it as you mature spiritually, as well as in your hospitality skills. Your prayer might read something like this:

> Gracious heavenly Father, thank you for your Word that challenges me to love both friends and strangers. Please help me to be excited about welcoming them into my home. Thank you for my home—may it always be a place of refuge, safety, protection, security, and refreshment for those who enter it. As well, I ask that it will be a center for evangelism in which I will at all times be ready to communicate the relationship I share with you to those who cross its threshold. Realizing that I cannot extend biblical hospitality without your strength, I ask that you empower me so that I am a useful vessel for your kingdom. Thank you for the material vessels you supplied—I consecrate each one to your service. I am grateful for the time and money to invest in this occasion. Please multiply both so that my guests will see your hand of provision.
>
> I request that my actions and words will be gracious, and that my guests would leave my home knowing more of you because they have spent time with me. Help me always to be careful to give you the praise for the positive results that come forth when I extend hospitality and to accept humbly your response of "no" when the requests I prayed for are not visible. Thank you for your love; help me to model it as I extend biblical hospitality. In your name I pray, amen.

The Invitation

Extend the invitation, keeping in mind that receiving an invitation in the mail is much more exciting than getting a phone call or an e-mail. Consider prayerfully whom our Lord would have you include on your guest list (review the contents of chapter 3).

Select a paper or invitation that communicates your theme. Make the message simple. Include your name, the occasion, date, time, RSVP deadline, and telephone number. An invitation's wording might look like this:

Pat Ennis
requests the honor of your presence
for afternoon tea at her home
Friday, May 29
at 2:00 p.m.
rsvp by May 25 to
661.234.5678

Remember that you may request an attendance response from your guests by adding the letters RSVP (French, *repondez, s'il vous plait*), meaning "the favor of a reply is requested," or simply including "regrets only by (insert the date)" if you care to know only if they are *not* accepting your invitation. Mail the invitations a minimum of two weeks in advance.

Prepare

Pray daily for the guests who will be attending. Craft your menu; a balance of sweet and savory is best (refer to the end of the chapter for tea recipes).[12] Select items that complement the season. If you plan to host a *full tea*, include on your menu a variety of tea sandwiches and fresh fruit. Follow with scones served with jams and clotted cream. Conclude with sweet desserts such as mini-tarts, cream puffs, and an assortment of cookies.

Prepare your spiritual menu. A primary reason for hostessing a *consecrated* china tea is the opportunity to introduce your guests to Christ and his Word. Both your tea and spiritual menu require careful crafting; for example, I have used the book of John and aligned spiritual truths with typical tea menu items:

- Sandwiches often have meat fillings—Jesus' meat was to complete the work his Father gave him to accomplish (John 4:31-34 KJV).
- Just as the jam and clotted cream enhance the taste of the scones, so Jesus enhances the life of the believer (John 10:10).
- Sweets are a reminder that God's Word should be more desired than honey or the honeycomb (Ps. 19:10).
- Tea's primary ingredient is water—Jesus is the living water (John 4:5–30).
- Grapes are frequently served at a tea. We know that they grow on vines; Jesus is the true vine. Those who have truly experienced salvation will bear evidence of being attached to the true vine by producing fruit (John 15:1, 5).
- Candles or "tea lights" are often used to illuminate the tea table—Jesus is the light of the world (John 8:12).

Once your spiritual menu is crafted, be sure to pray for opportunities to share your correlations.

Practice

Practice making a perfect pot of tea. Begin with freshly drawn *cold* water. Allow the cold water faucet to run several minutes to allow the water to fill with oxygen or use bottled or spring water. Avoid using distilled water since it lacks flavor. Heat the teapot by filling it with boiling water, allowing it to sit for a few minutes to warm the teapot, and then discarding it through the spout. Skipping this step will diminish the tea water's temperature and reduce the quality of the brewed tea.

Use one teaspoon of loose tea per cup plus an extra teaspoon "for the pot" (or one tea bag for two cups of brewed tea). Place loose tea in the pot, fabric tea sock, infusing basket, or paper filter. If you choose to use wire mesh balls, fill them no more than half full since they can cramp the leaves. This will allow the water to circulate around the leaves. When brewing herbal teas, use two teaspoons of tea for each eight ounces of water. Bring the water in a teakettle to a full *rolling* boil. Once the steam shoots straight up, pour the water over the leaves or bag(s) in the teapot. Dunking the tea bag in the water creates a mediocre pot of tea. Water that is not hot enough, as well as water that is overboiled (which causes the loss of oxygen) produces a flat tasting tea.

Immediately cover the teapot with the lid. Watch the clock rather than attempting to judge the tea strength by its color. A brewing rule of thumb is the larger the leaf, the longer the brewing time. Steep black teas three to five minutes; any longer can cause the tea to become bitter. Herbal teas may take more time, while green and oolong teas, because the leaves are more delicate, should be brewed one to three minutes with water that is slightly under the boiling point (bubbles are just beginning to form).

Strain the tea by removing the leaves or bags to prevent further steeping. Stir the tea and serve immediately. Keep unused tea warm in the teapot by placing the tea cozy (a padded covering used to maintain the heat in a teapot) onto the teapot. Place the tea cozy on the teapot *only after* the tea leaves are removed to prevent the tea from becoming bitter.

Get Organized

Develop a preparation schedule and a timetable that will enable you to enjoy the tea.

- Complete all of your shopping several days before the tea.
- Bake ahead and freeze scones and sweet desserts.
- Make only sandwiches that can be wrapped in plastic and stored in the refrigerator.
- Make a checklist so that you will remember to serve all of the tasty tea tidbits you created.
- Set the table the night before whenever possible.
- Commit the day of the tea to your heavenly Father, asking him to keep you calm (Phil. 4:6–7) so that you will be a gracious hostess (Prov. 11:16).[15]

Organize your consecrated vessels. Teas can be as formal or informal as you like. Some choose to use a formal tea service, others a mismatched collection of silverware and china. The rule of thumb is to select vessels that blend well together. An eclectic collection can stimulate conversation as you share with your guests how each vessel was acquired. Whether you choose an informal or formal tea, the following vessels are helpful:

- tea service (teapot, creamer, sugar bowl, and perhaps a vessel for holding artificial sweetener);
- cups, saucers, and small plates;
- infusers, i.e., strainers if loose tea is used (one is adequate, but individual ones are nice);
- teaspoons;
- butter knives;
- serving tray(s) for sandwiches;
- cake pedestals for sweets;
- basket for scones;
- serving tongs for each course;
- serving dishes and plates for butter, jam, and clotted cream.

Select and prepare the linens. Decide on the music—remember that complementary music adds a wonderful accompaniment to your tea while at the same time engaging another of the senses. Choose a centerpiece to match the linens and tea service. If your tea is formal, an assortment of freshly cut flowers in a silver or clear glass bowl is appropriate. A variety of centerpieces are suitable for an informal tea including a colored glass vase with flowers or a decorative glass bowl with floating flowers or candles.

If the tea is being served buffet-style, arrange the food in progression from savory to sweet. It is customary to serve a second beverage, in addition to tea, if the beverage preferences of the guests are unknown.

Consider sending your guests away with a small bag of After Tea Mints that provides them with a reminder of the pleasant, inspirational time they spent with you. As an herb, mint has been known for centuries for its cool, refreshing effect on the palate; our desire should be, when we entertain others, to have them depart from our presence physically and spiritually refreshed, so tucking some "spiritual after-tea mints" into the bag allows your guests to savor God's Word and the After Tea Mints at the same time. Activity 3 under *Practicing Hospitality* at the conclusion of this chapter provides you with the full instructions needed for this project.

Teatime Testimonies

Early in my Christian walk I read a book with a title something like *The 100 Percent Christian*. While I do not recall all of its contents, I do remember a key principle that made a significant impact on the way I live. The author spoke of how believers are to live as a witness to the Lord wherever they are. He then recounted the acclimation missionaries make when they arrive in a new location—they secure housing and transportation, locate a church, identify the sources for survival (groceries, etc.), and set about adjusting to the community. The author's focus was that all believers are missionaries, and wherever they live they have the same survival needs.

I have traveled vicariously with numbers of my alumnae as they have established residency in foreign countries—some single, others married. All have used their home economics training to minister to the women in the country of residence, and many have employed the international language of teatime as their vehicle. Two share their testimonies with us—Holly Nyquist and Sandy White. Tim and Holly Nyquist make their home in Bolivia, while Alan and Sandy White live in Turkey. Holly's contribution reflects the planning of a ladies' event at church, while Sandy reports a more intimate environment. Both offer the motivation and ideas for using our consecrated china wherever we may reside.

Dear Dr. Ennis,

I believe that ladies really love having teas because it draws us back to a time when we could just sit back, relax, renew, share, and enjoy the beauty around us that touches all of our senses.

When planning a tea try to think of all the senses—sight, sound, taste, touch, and hearing. During your planning meetings keep these in mind as you put together the details and make sure that every aspect is covered.

We have found that the best way to get ladies to come is by personal invitation. Our committee is made up of five women, each having their own connections to different groups of women in the community. Through this network we can invite a lot of people.

We also ask certain women to be table hostesses. A month before the actual tea we have a hostess brunch at the home of one of the committee members. During this time we introduce the theme of the tea and if possible the special speaker. This in turn gets the ladies excited and they begin to invite others.

Tickets are sold, which makes people committed to coming, three months in advance. With each passing month the price of the ticket is increased. We have planned enough teas that people know this so they try to purchase their tickets early. This helps us to know how many to expect at an early date.

As for the program, we have found that the ladies like variety. At the first few teas we had the usual special song followed by the speaker, but we have had more positive comments when we presented a variety in the program: skits, poems, demonstrating how to do a craft, door prizes, live music, a men's quartet, and special instrumentals—all at the same tea! Yes, it is a lot of work, but word gets around that these teas are not something you want to miss (unless there is civil unrest and a four-day weekend☺!). If the ladies can bring their daughters we tend to have a larger attendance. I believe it is because there are so few activities to do here with children that more people come.

The planning—we finally sat down after a year of doing this and sifted through which ideas to repeat, what to add, and what to eliminate. Christmas and Mother's Day teas are ones that people make a special effort to attend. We found that it was best to have a tea every three to four months during the school year and to announce the next date sometime during the one in progress. We have a planning meeting almost every other week until the last month when we have one every week. The two biggest time consumers are selling the tickets and the program. We try to establish a theme and then provide the decorations to enhance the mood.

We always end with the gospel message. There are forms that we place on each of the tables that request the guests' names, phone numbers, and comments, and a place to indicate if they accepted Christ that day. The committee follows up on the completed forms.

Love and prayers,
Holly Nyquist

Dear Dr. Ennis:

I have been giving some thought to your request. Tea really is a big part of the life in Turkey. I see that tea parties are a large part of my life here because it builds relationships and helps me to understand the culture better. I've done a few teatimes where we have also done crafts and were able to share a bit of the gospel with guests. Evangelism has to be lower key here and relationships are important. In order to build relationships I have participated in many "gold teas"; they are very popular.

Usually nine or ten women agree to meet together, usually once a month, and the event moves from home to home so each member has one party in her home. The hostess provides the refreshments, and each guest gives the hostess a gold coin (right now each gold coin is worth about thirty dollars). This is an acceptable way to have an intimate part in the lives of these ladies since they see the tea as a great way of helping one another. A woman can request that the next tea be in her home and then she can collect the gold and use it for an emergency expense. It is also a time when the ladies give each other moral support and get some handwork done.

Basically the teatimes come down to helping, being a friend, and belonging to something that meets the needs of the ladies here . . . but isn't it the same everywhere?

Love,
Sandy White[16]

As you consider Holly's and Sandy's teatime testimonies it is my prayer that you will be motivated to consecrate your china to our Lord's use today—wherever you reside—so that you too may have a part in helping other women to "taste and see that the LORD is good!"

A Concluding Consideration

Exemplifying spiritual and physical consecration of our hospitality skills and resources requires time and effort. To coordinate or "dovetail" the two, consider using the Spiritual Entertainment Timetable on the following page as you prepare for your guests.

TABLE 5.1

Spiritual Entertainment Timetable

Spiritually I will	as I physically
Thank my heavenly Father that I am included on the guest list for the marriage supper of the Lamb (Rev. 19:7).	Prepare my guest list.
Bring to mind God's providential care of me (Ps. 104:27; 136:25; 145:15–16).	Create my menu.
Evaluate my use of time in relation to the brevity of life (Ps. 90:12).	Prepare my time schedule.
Recall that I was purchased with a price (1 Cor. 6:19–20).	Grocery shop.
Bring to mind that God gave Moses specific instructions for the table appointments for the tabernacle including the color of the table linens (Num. 4:7–10).	Decide on my table linens.
Focus on being a vessel of honor (2 Tim. 2:21).	Select my table appointments (china, silver, glassware, etc.).
Examine my heart to ensure that it is clean (Ps. 24:4; 51:10).	Make certain that all of my table appointments are spotless.
Remind myself of Christ's sacrifice for me (Luke 24:44–47).	Sacrifice my time and energy to clean my home and prepare the meal.
Reflect on Christ's example of servanthood (John 13:1–20).	Serve my guests.
Model the speech of the wise woman (Prov. 31:26).	Intentionally direct the conversation in wholesome avenues.
Think about the process of cleansing from sin (1 John 1:7, 9).	Tidy my home after the event.

Practicing Hospitality

1. Acquaint yourself with the examples of biblical men and women who provided refreshment for those who communicated the gospel. Create and complete a chart like the one that follows.

Biblical Example	Scripture Reference and Truth Taught	Practical Ways I Can Follow This Example
Lazarus, Mary, and Martha	Luke 10:38–42 Truth taught: Martha welcomed Jesus into her home. (I am providing one example to get you started.)	Make my home available to others.
Sarah	Genesis 18; Hebrews 13:2 Truth taught:	
Esther	Esther 5 Truth taught:	
The wise woman of Proverbs	Proverbs 31:10–31 Truth taught:	
Simon the tanner	Acts 9:35–10:23; Hebrews 13:2; 3 John 5–8 Truth taught:	
Lydia	Acts 16:15; Romans 12:13; 1 Peter 4:9; 3 John 8 Truth taught:	

2. Craft your own Prayer of Consecration; write out the prayer, review it each time you entertain, and modify it as you mature spiritually, as well as in your hospitality skills.

3. Use the After Tea Mints recipes located at the end of this chapter or purchase some tasty mints, along with small, decorative party bags. Using pretty paper and an attractive computer font or hand printing, create "spiritual after-tea mints" (choice tidbits to chew on and digest that produce a mouth that is always pleasant). Add a note that thanks your guests for attending and encourages them to meditate on the spiritual after-tea mints. Some verses to consider using

include Psalm 107:1; Proverbs 18:2; 31:26; 1 Corinthians 13:1, 4, 6; Ephesians 4:32; Philippians 4:6, 8, 12–13; 1 Thessalonians 5:18; 1 Timothy 6:6; and James 3:2, 5, 10.

4. Use the table below as a model to develop your personal "Spiritual Entertainment Timetable."

My Spiritual Entertainment Timetable

Verse	Action
Revelation 19:7	Include a variety of people on my guest list.
Psalm 104:27; 136:25; 145:15–16	
Psalm 90:12	
1 Corinthians 6:19–20	
Proverbs 31:22	
2 Timothy 2:21	
Psalm 24:4; 51:10	
Luke 24:44–47	
John 13:1–20	
Proverbs 31:26	
1 John 1:7, 9	

5. Plan a simple, basic Bible study that could be used to introduce others to Christ; then pray that our heavenly Father will provide you with an opportunity to use it. Include:

- Scripture references;
- organizational details—length of time for each session, format (prayer, music, refreshments, etc.);
- questions to ask that stimulate discussion of the content taught;
- homework assignments;
- supplementary resources.

Recipe Resources

Practice hospitality by selecting several recipes from the selection below that you can bake and freeze. Pray for opportunities to use them with your consecrated china—remember they can be as simple as a scone and a cup of tea with a neighbor or as elaborate as a Victorian tea. Select the occasion to align with your season of life—but do plan to use your consecrated china soon!

After Tea Mints

2 cups granulated sugar
½ cup water
½ cup light corn syrup
⅛ teaspoon cream of tartar
a few drops flavored oil
food coloring

Cook granulated sugar, water, and light corn syrup in 2-quart saucepan; stir till sugar dissolves. Cook to thread stage (232 degrees) without stirring. Add cream of tartar; beat with wire whip till creamy. Add a few drops flavored oil and food coloring. Drop from teaspoon onto waxed paper forming patties. (Keep pan over hot water.) Store tightly covered.

Makes about 60

Cranberry Scones

3 cups all-purpose flour
2½ teaspoons baking powder
¾ teaspoon salt
¾ cup dried cranberries
1 cup buttermilk
⅓ cup sugar
½ teaspoon baking soda
¾ cup chilled butter (1½ sticks)
1 teaspoon grated orange zest

Preheat oven to 400 degrees. Mix dry ingredients. Add chilled butter; beat together with electric mixer. Add cranberries and orange zest. Pour in buttermilk and mix well (may need to knead with your hands a bit; looks dry at first).

Divide dough in half and form balls. Roll out into 2 circles ½–¼-inch thick. Cut each circle into 8 wedges. Bake for 12–15 minutes or until golden brown.

Makes 16 scones

Easy Devonshire Cream

1 3-ounce package cream cheese
1 tablespoon and ¾ teaspoon white sugar
1¼ pinches salt
1¼ cups heavy cream

In a medium bowl, cream together cream cheese, sugar, and salt. Beat in cream until stiff peaks form. Chill until serving time.[17]

Raspberry Cream Cheese

3 ounces cream cheese, softened
1½ tablespoons raspberry preserves

Stir cream cheese and preserves in a small bowl until combined. Serve immediately or cover and refrigerate. Let stand at room temperature for 15 minutes to soften after refrigeration.

Makes about ½ cup

Almond Chicken Tea Sandwiches

6 boneless chicken breasts, cooked and chopped
  coarsely
1 cup slivered, blanched almonds
1 cup mayonnaise
butter
1 loaf white or wheat sandwich bread

Mix chicken, almonds, and mayonnaise. Butter each slice of bread well. On half the slices, spoon about 3 tablespoons of almond chicken mixture. Top with remaining slices.

Stack three sandwiches tall. Wrap in waxed paper and again in a slightly dampened kitchen towel. Let set for at least one hour. Unwrap, cut off crusts, and cut into triangles.

Makes 36 sandwiches

Lady Laura's Favorite Tea Punch

Graciously shared by the Tea Lady, Laura Leathers[18]

2 cups sugar
4 cups water
juice of 4 fresh lemons
1 cup strong tea
1 tablespoon vanilla extract
1 tablespoon almond extract
1 2-liter bottle ginger ale, chilled

Boil sugar, water, and lemon juice for 3 minutes. Cool. Combine with tea, vanilla, and almond extract. Immediately before serving, add ginger ale and pour over chipped ice.

Makes 1 gallon

Elegant Cucumber Rounds
(A cucumber is always to be served at a tea party)
Graciously shared by the Tea Lady, Laura Leathers

1 large cucumber
1 teaspoon salt
1 tablespoon white vinegar
1 (8-ounce) package cream cheese, softened
1½ teaspoons mayonnaise
⅛ teaspoon seasoned salt
1 loaf multi-grain bread
parsley sprigs

Peel cucumber. Cut cucumber in half horizontally. Peel, seed, and place in a bowl. Add the salt and vinegar, and fill bowl with cold water. Cover bowl and set aside for 1 to 2 hours.

Empty cucumber halves into colander; rinse well with cold tap water and let drain. Pat dry with paper towels. Shred or finely chop half of cucumber. Measure ⅓ cup shredded cucumber. Slice remaining cucumber for garnish.

Combine cream cheese, mayonnaise, and seasoned salt, mixing until well blended. Stir in shredded cucumber. Cut two 2-inch rounds from each bread slice. Spread each round with 1 teaspoon cucumber spread. Garnish each sandwich with half slice of cucumber and a sprig of parsley.

Makes 48 sandwiches

Egg Salad on Egg Bread

3 hard-boiled eggs, peeled, finely chopped
½ cup mayonnaise (don't use "lite" mayonnaise)
1 tablespoon finely chopped green onion
salt and pepper to taste
10 slices egg bread

Mix ingredients until well combined. Spread the bread with a thin coating of mayonnaise. Spread with the egg salad. After making each sandwich, cut off crusts, and cut into three parallel sections.

Makes 30 sandwiches

6

Hospitality and OTHERS

What good is it, my brothers, if someone says he has faith but does not have works? Can that faith save him? If a brother or sister is poorly clothed and lacking in daily food, and one of you says to them, "Go in peace, be warmed and filled," without giving them the things needed for the body, what good is that?

—JAMES 2:14–16

Several years ago I read "The Boxcar Wall," a devotional that put the principle of James 2:14–16 in perspective for me:

I ate breakfast the other day with a man who 60 years ago sold newspapers and shined shoes on the streets of downtown Boise, Idaho. He told me about his life in those days and how much things have changed. "What's changed the most?" I asked him. "People," he said. "They don't care anymore."

As a case in point, he told me about his mother, who often fed hungry men who came to her house. Every day she prepared food for her family and then made several more meals because she knew homeless travelers would start to show up around mealtime. She had deep compassion for those who were in need. Once she asked a man how he happened to find his way to her door. "Your address is written on all the boxcar walls," he said.[1]

As you concentrate on applying James 2:14–16 to your life, you will want to consider the "others" to whom you could minister—singles, widows, the grieving, the hospitalized, those with dietary challenges, individuals experiencing food insecurity (those with low incomes, those at poverty level, the homeless), as well as the elderly. To apply this passage effectively you must first understand the characteristics of biblical compassion.

Biblical Compassion: What Is It?

"In those days, when again a great crowd had gathered, and they had nothing to eat, he called his disciples to him and said to them, 'I have compassion on the crowd, because they have been with me now three days and have nothing to eat'" (Mark 8:1–2). Jessica Nelson North penned a little poem, "Three Guests," that captures the twenty-first-century attitude toward hospitality and its relationship to compassion:

> I gave a little tea party
> This afternoon at three.
> 'Twas very small,
> Three guests in all—
> I, myself, and me.
> Myself ate up the sandwiches
> While I drank all the tea,
> 'Twas also I
> Who ate the pie
> And passed the cake to me.[2]

You see, hospitality is not about you and me. As a matter of fact, when your ego gets involved you are definitely missing the primary reason for hospitality. John Ruskin writes, "When a man is all wrapped up in himself he makes a pretty small package."[3] I have an idea that the same description applies to women. Let's craft an equation that helps us understand the relationship between hospitality and compassion using the definition of both words:

THE FRIENDLY RECEPTION AND TREATMENT OF GUESTS OR STRANGERS[4]

+

A FEELING OF DEEP SYMPATHY AND SORROW FOR SOMEONE STRUCK BY
MISFORTUNE, ACCOMPANIED BY
A DESIRE TO ALLEVIATE THE SUFFERING[5]

=

COMPASSIONATE HOSPITALITY

The Compassionate Hospitality Equation moves you from an *I* to an *others* focus. As believers, we know that one of the attributes of our heavenly Father's character is compassion. As his children our compassion should include a sense of empathy for the distress of others (Rom. 9:15), coupled with the desire to minimize the distress (Matt. 9:36; 14:14; 15:32; 18:27; 20:34; Mark 1:41; 6:34; 8:2; 9:22; Luke 7:13; 10:33; 15:20), as well as a heart that demonstrates kindness and mercy to others (Matt. 18:33; Mark 5:19; Jude 22). Graciousness, longsuffering, an abundance of goodness and truth, delayed anger, and great mercy (Ex. 34:6–7; Ps. 86:15; 145:8), are additional qualities of our heavenly Father's character that should typify our behavior. Through his strength, if you make his compassion yours, your Compassionate Hospitality Equation will move away from being ego-centered, will be directed toward the needs of others rather than your own, and, most importantly, it will reflect his character. The complete biblical Compassionate Hospitality Equation might look something like this:

THE FRIENDLY RECEPTION AND TREATMENT OF GUESTS OR STRANGERS
MOTIVATED BY THE LONGING TO DEMONSTRATE BIBLICAL KINDNESS
AND LOVE

+

A SENSE OF EMPATHY FOR THE DISTRESS OF OTHERS COUPLED
WITH THE DESIRE TO MINIMIZE THAT DISTRESS AND DEMONSTRATE
KINDNESS AND MERCY

=

COMPASSIONATE HOSPITALITY

Joseph Stowell offers a concise description of biblical compassion:

> Several words are used in Scripture to translate our English word *compassion*. Their meanings in both Hebrew and Greek are highly instructive. Two basic words are used in the Old Testament, one of which means "to bear, to become responsible for, to spare someone from trouble." This Hebrew word deals mainly with our actions. The second Hebrew term is more attitudinal. It means "to be soft, gentle." It is sometimes translated "womb" and also means to "be wide" in encompassing others and their needs.
>
> The leading word for compassion in the New Testament means "that emotion aroused by contact with affliction." It is the Greek word used to translate the Old Testament concept of God's loyal, unfailing covenant love. The stress in this particular word is on the action that flows out of our being as we are touched by another's affliction. In fact, the difference between sympathy and biblical compassion is that biblical compassion—true compassion—always leads to action. Compassion is not measured by how we feel but by what we do in response to how we feel.[6]

While we often think of hospitality and compassion as inviting someone to our home for meals or lodging, a journey through Scripture introduces us to individuals who chose to extend compassionate hospitality in a variety of ways.

Pharaoh's daughter chose to extend long-term hospitality to baby Moses (Ex. 2:6–10). Shobi brought beds, basins, vessels, and sheep to David and his people while they were in exile (2 Sam. 17:27–29). Elijah restored the life of the widow's son—a relationship that was cultivated because she chose, out of her need, to share with him (1 Kings 17:18–24). Nehemiah wept, mourned, prayed, and fasted for Jerusalem and its citizens (Neh. 1:1–11). Job's friends traveled from their homes to mourn with and comfort him in his pain (Job 2:11–13). Job wept for those in trouble and grieved for the poor (Job 30:25). David displayed sympathy to those who falsely accused him (Ps. 35:13–14). The Jews came to comfort Mary and Martha at Lazarus's death (John 11:19). Paul communicated the gospel message to all classes of people—Jew and Gentile alike (1 Cor. 9:22).

The Lord Jesus, having experienced physical hunger, empathized with the hunger of others (Matt. 4:2). He offered rest to the spiritually bankrupt (Matt. 11:28–30); he brought comfort and encouragement to the weak and oppressed (Isa. 40:11; 42:3; Matt. 12:18–21); he ministered to physical and spiritual needs (Matt. 14:13–21; Mark 6:31–44; 8:2; Luke 9:11–17; John 6:1–13); he attended to the afflicted (Luke 7:13; John 11:33, 35); he alleviated the plight of the diseased (Mark 1:41); he offered hope to perishing sinners (Matt. 9:36; Luke 19:41; John 3:16); and he modeled a necessary character quality for those in spiritual leadership (Heb. 5:2, 7).

Putting your scriptural journey in practical terms, if you are going to exhibit compassionate hospitality you will consider:

- nurturing the abandoned;
- providing material needs;
- weeping, mourning, praying, and, when appropriate, fasting for others;
- sharing your faith with the spiritually bankrupt;
- encouraging the weak and oppressed;
- assisting with the needs of the infirm; and
- modeling biblical compassion.

I began this section with Jessica Nelson North's little poem "Three Guests" and suggested that it characterized the twenty-first-century attitude toward hospitality and its relationship to compassion—even among believers. It is my prayer that our study of biblical compassion has challenged you to move from the ego-centered reasons for extending hospitality to the compassionate motivations expressed by the Lord; then perhaps your attitude will be more like the thoughts expressed here in "Compassionate Hospitality" than those in "Three Guests":

> I gave a little dinner party
> this evening at six.
> The guests were such a blessing—
> I really enjoyed the mix.
> The widow shared her wisdom,
> the single her homeless ministry,
> the young couple their vision for working with trou-
> bled teens
> and I my passion for meeting women's special needs.
> As we ate and prayed together,
> (two staples of biblical hospitality)
> our hearts were filled with compassion
> and the desire to impact eternity!

Hospitality as a Way of Displaying Compassion

"The King will answer them, 'Truly, I say to you, as you did it to one of the least of these my brothers, you did it to me'" (Matt. 25:40). Your opportunities to use hospitality as a way of displaying compassion are literally limitless, but to get you started let's target several categories of people—singles, widows, the grieving, the hospitalized, those with dietary challenges, individuals experiencing food insecurity (low-income, poverty-level, or homeless), and the elderly.

Singles

Single is defined as "pertaining to the unmarried state."[7] The October 20, 2003, cover story of *Business Week* reports:

> The U.S. Census Bureau's newest numbers show that married-couple households—the dominant cohort since the country's founding—have slipped from nearly 80% in the 1950s to just 50.7% today. That means that the U.S.'s 86 million single adults could soon define the new majority. Already, unmarrieds make up 42% of the workforce, 40% of homebuyers, 35% of voters, and one of the most potent—if pluralistic—consumer groups on record.[8]

Since singles are a part of the Christian community, consider how they impact your application of hospitality and compassion from two perspectives—the single as an invited guest and the single as the initiator of guests.

The Single as an Invited Guest

When I was a faculty member at Christian Heritage College the Lord graciously provided me with a lovely home—and it happened to be just the right size to entertain the entire faculty of the college, most of whom were married. I made an interesting observation as multiple events were held at my home: the couples arrived and left together and sometimes sat together during the meal or refreshment time. The remainder of the time the ladies were generally clustered together in one part of the living room, the men in another. They were essentially functioning as unmarried people while at the event, but the majority of the couples present would not invite a single person to an event they were hosting.

As you consider your guest lists, consider the singles you know who could be included. More than likely their life experiences are rich, and they will enhance your social gathering.

165

The Single as the Initiator of Guests

My friend Nancy Leigh DeMoss writes:

> Those of us who are single face a danger of becoming self-absorbed. Free from the constraints of family life, it is all too easy to become preoccupied with fulfilling our own social needs or consumed with our jobs or with making money. Now, there's certainly nothing wrong with having friends or careers or making a living, but God is concerned about the heart motives of His children. Rather than devoting their lives to furthering the Kingdom of Christ, many Christian singles have been caught in the trap of self-seeking and self-fulfillment.[9]

Placing Nancy's statement in the context of hospitality and compassion, singles have the freedom and, yes, the gift for a season of their lives (1 Cor. 7:32–35) to minister to others in a unique way. Often the single's discretionary time is greater than that of women with families. The season of singleness is a great time to practice all of those recipes that can become family favorites if you marry and to develop the hospitality skills that may well position you to offer the biblical hospitality required of those in church leadership (1 Tim. 3:2; Titus 1:8).

If you are single, partner with a friend to practice working as a team—you can't lose. If the Lord has chosen you to be single for just a season, you are much better prepared for a partner than living in a state of limbo until the right person comes along. If your gift of singleness is for a lifetime, you have not wasted valuable time. I did not wait for marriage to practice hospitality and compassion. If I had waited, I would have missed hundreds of opportunities to minister to others!

Nancy also encourages singles to become involved in the lives of families and offers wonderful counsel to singles and couples alike:

I have discovered that regular involvement with families is a safeguard against selfishness. And for those who will one day be married, there is hardly any better preparation for marriage and parenting. In a family setting, we can witness firsthand the blessing of obeying God's plan for the home and the consequences of disregarding it. Nothing will rid us of unrealistic notions of marriage and parenting faster than in-depth involvement in real homes.

When singles are assimilated into families, everyone benefits. The single adult can have a strong spiritual influence on children that reinforces the training provided by their parents. Singles can meet needs of parents, such as to have time alone without the children. Families can provide friendship and encouragement to singles. Both families and singles can offer each other mutual support, counsel, accountability, and prayer.

On a practical note, I have known single men and women who would love to spend time with families and become resentful when families don't think to reach out to them. My personal experience is that most married couples are not aware of the value of including singles in the life of their family, and therefore generally don't take the initiative to do so. So my challenge to singles is this: don't be afraid to reach out to families! Look for ways to initiate relationships with children, young people, and couples, as well as older people who are alone and in need of families.[10]

Widows

A widow is "a woman who has lost her husband by death and has not remarried."[11] National Bereavement Statistics reported by the American Association of Retired People (AARP) tell us:

- Almost 2 million persons celebrated their 65th birthday in 1999—that's 5,422 birthdays per day. In the same year, 1.8 million persons 65 and older died, resulting in a net increase of the 65-and-older population by approximately 200,000 (558) per day. (National Center for Health Statistics, 2000).

- In 1999 almost half (45%) of the women over 65 were widows. Nearly 700,000 women lose their husbands each year and will be widows for an average of 14 years (U.S. Bureau of the Census).
- The average monthly benefit for non-disabled widow(er)s was $812 in February 2000 (Social Security Administration).
- In 1999 there were over four times as many widows (8.4 million) as widowers (1.9 million).[12]

Scripture provides a clear definition of a Christian widow and specific instructions on how the church is to respond to her if she has no means of providing for her daily needs. A Christian widow, according to 1 Timothy 5:3–16, is one who is sixty years or older (in the New Testament culture sixty was considered retirement age) (5:9a); was totally devoted and faithful to her husband and who displayed purity of thought and action during her marriage (5:9b); is a Christian mother who reared children that followed the Lord (5:10a); is willing to perform humble acts of service (5:10b); and is known for her good works (5:10c).

The church is instructed to nurture widows by doing good works for them (Isa. 1:17); honoring them (1 Tim. 5:3); encouraging their family to provide for their needs (1 Tim. 5:4, 16); providing for their daily needs if they lack financial resources (Acts 6:1; 1 Tim. 5:9); visiting them (James 1:27); and allowing them to share in blessings (Deut. 14:29; 16:11, 14; 24:19–21).

Because widows comprise a significant portion of the Christian community, consider how they impact the integration of hospitality and compassion from two perspectives—the widow as an invited guest and the widow as the initiator of guests.

The Widow as an Invited Guest

I was eighteen when my mother became a widow. As a college freshman I not only had to deal with my own grief, but I also was faced with the responsibility of helping her to adjust to a new lifestyle. You see, when Dad died, she not only lost her husband of thirty years, but she also lost her circle of friends. Suddenly the married couples (my dad was the first of their group to die) didn't know what to do about Mother, so they did nothing. Her grieving process was actually extended because of the withdrawal of her friends, many with whom she and Dad had enjoyed fellowship for years.

As with the single, the widow possesses a wealth of life experiences that will enhance your social gathering. In the beginning of her grieving process she may not be the life of the party, but your invitation, extended with a heart of compassion, may allow her recovery process to accelerate. Remember, as believers we are instructed to be sensitive and compassionate to the pain and sorrows of others (Rom. 12:15; Col. 3:12)- -and there is a 50/50 chance that one day you will be in the same situation (Gal. 6:7)![13]

The Widow as the Initiator of Guests

There is a happy ending to my mother's loss of her circle of friends! Ever the gracious southern hostess, she did not cease to extend hospitality because of the change in her marital status. In the five years that she lived beyond Dad's death, Mom and I entertained frequently, and eventually our guest list included widows from the group that had earlier excluded my mother. Though her arthritic condition precluded her engaging in as much of the food preparation as she was accustomed to doing, she continued to help me hone the skills that were second nature to her.

The night before she stepped into the presence of our Lord, she prepared a special meal to welcome my friend Carella to our home. As a widow, my mother chose to be an initiator of guests rather than to isolate herself or marinate in self-pity, and in so doing, she left an immeasurable legacy to me.

The Grieving

Grieving individuals are an interesting dichotomy: generally they desperately need nourishment but have no desire to eat. Having lost both of my parents, I can attest to the blessing that hospitality provides to those who are grieving. Following are some tips to consider when engaging in this practical application of Romans 12:15.

Remember that the grieving are probably tired, sensitive, hungry, and often tense; plan a meal with protein, fresh fruits and vegetables, breads, and a light dessert since such a menu will assist in defusing some of these emotions. Refrain from serving foods that contain high quantities of caffeine, nitrates, preservatives, or large amounts of sugar or salt, since these ingredients can increase stress levels.

Consult the person, a family member, or someone close to the family to determine what type of hospitality best suits her needs. As with other forms of hospitality, determine if there are specific dietary constraints that should be considered.

Impart emotional support along with the physical food. Simply delivering the food can communicate that you are purely fulfilling an obligatory service. Your goal is to mix compassion with consumption. Carry the food in containers that do not need to be returned. Provide any necessary preparation instructions. Arrange the food aesthetically. While the grieving may not feel like eating, an attractive presentation may stimulate their appetite.

Finally, remember the grieving once the final services are completed. A myriad of lonely days will undoubtedly stretch before them. Invite them to lunch or coffee, and include them in holiday celebrations. They may choose to decline the invitations initially, but as the early pain recedes they will one day be ready to say, "Yes, I would love to come."

As we fulfill Romans 12:15, more often than not we will find that we have provided a ministry of compassion that no restaurant or catered meal could.

Hospital Hospitality

My first stay in the hospital occurred in the middle of my doctoral examinations. Having written for a four-hour time increment (one of four) without moving from my chair, I was not surprised that I felt a bit cramped when I stood up. However, the discomfort did not subside, and several days later I found myself in the hospital for gall bladder surgery. Regrettably, this was before laser surgery. I had been in a hospital multiple times to visit a parent or friends; these experiences, coupled with my own hospital stay, taught me some important and helpful lessons on how to provide hospital hospitality to both the patient and her family.

The Family

As with the grieving, the family with a hospitalized member is probably tired, sensitive, hungry, and often tense. Consider taking a basket meal filled with tasty items, attractively prepared, consisting of protein, fresh fruits and vegetables, breads, and a light dessert that will assist in defusing some of these emotions. Check with the family to ensure that your provision is a help, not a hindrance. Carry the food in containers that do not need to be returned.

Offer to stay with the patient for a while so the family can take a break, run errands, or consume the contents of the tasty basket you prepared. Another idea is to provide gift cards to restaurants. Send cards and notes of encouragement to the family as well as to the patient. Prepare a package of thank-you notes; either the family or the patient can use them. Include stamps as well. Remember that often the family's real work occurs when the patient returns home. Continue to extend hospitality and compassion during the recovery period.

The Patient

Remember that the patient is in the hospital to take advantage of the services that it provides, so don't allow your presence to encumber the work of hospital personnel.

Call before you visit the first time to discern whether visitors are appropriate. Send cards early and often; keeping a supply of cards and stamps on hand will prevent procrastination. If the patient is a visual person, as I am, the cards and notes you write will provide encouragement during the "valley experiences."

If the room has a phone, purchase a long distance phone card for the patient. As she improves, your gift may allow her to keep in touch with the real world. Offer to read Scripture or pray when you visit; leaving her with a verse written on a card can provide a source of meditation during some of the dark hours when everyone has gone home.

Most hospital rooms will have more than one patient in them—be sensitive to the roommate's needs, as well. Keep your visit short; however, allow the patient to talk about her experiences if she wishes. Often she will want to think about something other than her plight, so be ready to share uplifting thoughts with her.

Include your children, whenever possible. Elizabeth Gilbert, the mother of thirteen children, writes about the intentional involvement of her children in hospital hospitality:

> Our family enjoys ministering in the area of music. We continue to develop the gift God has given us. We have sung in our church and mom has played some offertories. Justin and Joseph bless us on their harmonicas harmonizing so nicely. We've had the opportunity to be a blessing in nursing homes and to various shut-ins and to patients in the hospitals.
>
> We believe in ministering with cards and letters as a means of hospitality. Again the idea of ministering of one's substance is the idea (key). Some things children can learn from writing letters are: proper writing skills/techniques, care for others (the Golden Rule), and creativity![14]

Finally, don't forget about the patient when she goes home. Often the hospitalized patient is inundated with company and then is isolated when she is released. Even if you can't visit as easily, call periodically. Then when she is ready to reenter the world, invite her to your home. The section that follows may provide you with some ideas for how to deal with her potential dietary needs.

Guests with Dietary Challenges

Health, United States is an annual report of national trends in health statistics.[15] The 2003 edition provides sobering facts about the nutritional habits of individuals living in America:

- The prevalence of obesity among adults twenty to seventy-four years of age increased from 47 percent in 1976–1980 to 65 percent in 1999–2000.
- During this period the prevalence of obesity among adults twenty to seventy-four years of age increased from 15 to 28 percent.
- Between 1976–1980 and 1999–2000 the prevalence of obesity among children six to eleven years of age more than doubled from 7 to 15 percent.
- During the same time increment, the prevalence of obesity among adolescents twelve to nineteen years of age more than tripled from 5 to 16 percent.

Given these statistics there is a good possibility that you, someone in your family, your guests, or those to whom you provide "portable hospitality" will have dietary constraints. Let's consider some guidelines in graciously meeting these constraints.

If you have dietary constraints or food allergies, share them with your hostess when you are invited. It is very discouraging for a hostess to spend time preparing for her guests, only to find they are unable to partake in the menu items.

173

As a hostess, inquire if the guest has dietary constraints or food allergies when you extend the invitation. This can be done tactfully by saying something like, "Are there any foods which you prefer to exclude from your diet?"

Gather some facts about food allergies. An Internet search is a great start in collecting resources. I did an Internet search that took 0.14 seconds and gave me 2,240 different sources of information on food allergies—and I never left home or purchased a book.

Learn to garnish. Attractive presentation adds "plate appeal" to a menu that may appear boring. Expose your family to a variety of types of diets as a normal part of your menu planning. Table 6.1 presents some common dietary constraints people encounter—low fat, vegetarian, and diabetic. Along with their descriptions, several sample menus are included, and the recipes are found at the end of this chapter. All of the menus are tasty, and if your family cultivates their palates for a variety of kinds of food they will not be shocked if they are suddenly served a meal that is somewhat bland.

TABLE 6.1

Common Dietary Constraints

Dietary Constraint	Description	Suggested Menu
Low fat	• Total fat intake should be no more than 30% of the daily calorie intake.	Mixed Green Salad Chicken Cacciatore Brown Rice Angel Food Cake with Fruit Glaze
	• Saturated fat should not exceed 10% of the **total** fat intake.	Raspberry Iced Tea Coffee/Iced Water with Lemon
	• Cholesterol should be kept under 300 mg per day.	Tossed Green Salad Crock-Pot Beef Chili with Non-fat Cheese Cornbread Muffins with Honey Orange-Baked Apples Orange Pekoe Iced Tea Iced Water with Lemon Coffee/Hot Tea

Dietary Constraint	Description	Suggested Menu
Vegetarian	A variety of vegetarian diets exist:	*Lacto-vegetarian* Greek Village Salad
	1. *Semi-vegetarian—* dairy products, eggs, chicken, and fish are allowed, but no other types of meat.	Vegetarian Lentils, Pasta, and Rice Creamy Pudding with Berries Hot Earl Grey Tea Iced Water with Lemon
	2. *Pesco-vegetarian—* dairy products, eggs, and fish only.	*Semi-vegetarian* Vegetarian Combo Pizza Spinach Salad
	3. *Lacto-vegetarian—* dairy products, no meat or eggs.	Pineapple Strawberry Ice Iced Water with Lemon Coffee or Hot Tea
	4. *Ovo-vegetarian—*no dairy products or meat, but eggs are allowed.	
	5. *Vegetarian—*no animal products are consumed.	
	6. *Lacto-ovo-vegetarian—*animal products, but no meat.	
Diabetic	1. No sugar in any form is allowed in the diet.	Fruit Salad
	2. Carbohydrates should not comprise more than 55% of the daily calories.	Chicken Nut Stir Fry Macaroni and Cheese Warm Apple Cinnamon Cobbler Hot Tea
	3. Protein should be limited to 20%.	Iced Water with Lemon
	4. Total fat intake should be no more than 25% of the daily calorie intake.	French Onion Soup Poached Beef Tenderloin Stuffed Artichokes with Carrots
	5. Saturated fat should not exceed 10% of the total fat intake.	Raspberry Sorbet Coffee/Iced Water with Lemon
	6. Cholesterol should be less than 300 mg.	
	7. Sodium, no more than 3 grams per day.	
	8. Follow exchange list to select foods to meet daily food requirements.[16]	

Compassion and Food Security

Food Security is a twenty-first-century term that describes whether an individual has access, at all times, to enough food for an active, healthy life. You are more than likely familiar with terms like *low income*, *poverty level*, or *the homeless*, which describe *food insecurity*. This term should touch the hearts of believers when they consider that the Lord Jesus, during his earthly ministry, was in essence a homeless person (Matt. 8:20; 2 Cor. 8:9). According to the USDA *Hunger Report*:

- 89% of American households were *food secure* throughout 2002.
- The remaining households were *food insecure* for at least some time during that year.
- The prevalence of *food insecurity* rose from 10.7 percent in 2001 to 11.1 percent in 2002, while the prevalence of *food insecurity* with hunger rose from 3.3 percent to 3.5 percent.[17]

While our pantries may not always be filled with all of the delicacies that our palate desires, most of us have an adequate enough food supply to be considered *food secure*; therefore, we can demonstrate hospitality and compassion by designating a portion of our food budget each month to those who encounter *food insecurity*. You may ask, "What would I buy, or how would I begin?" If your church has a program in place, consider supporting it; if not, begin by researching what programs your local community might have. For example, I did an Internet search about the community where I live and found a web site for the Food Pantry. It provided a list of needed food and non-food items that can be a helpful resource for assembling a bag of groceries to share with others:

Food Items

peanut butter	pasta	macaroni and cheese
canned vegetables	canned fruit	canned beans
canned meat	tuna	dried beans and rice
soup (canned or dry)	cereal	dry milk
cooking oil	jelly/jam	baby food

Non-food Items

diapers (larger sizes)	toothpaste	shampoo
laundry detergent	bar soap	household cleansers[18]
feminine hygiene products	deodorant	

While we may lack the resources to purchase a full bag of groceries, we can probably manage several items—even if it means excluding the ice cream or chips from our grocery list. Perhaps you can collect the items for several weeks and then make a trip to the distribution center of your choice to apply hospitality and compassion in a practical way.

Sharing our time and other resources at an agency at which the primary purpose is to meet the needs of the food insecure is another way to practice compassion and hospitality. Again, an Internet search provided me with a description of some of the needs of a typical Rescue Mission during the holiday season. Meal packers and deliverers volunteer to pack meals or use their vehicles to deliver meals to folks who are homebound due to illness or age. What a good family activity!

Kitchen helpers comprised of groups and individuals help with advance preparations for holiday meals during the months of November and December. Decorators are needed, and they come to brighten the Rescue Mission campus for the holidays. Others are needed to bake four hundred fruit pies for holiday meals, and three hundred dozen cookies, such as chocolate chip, sugar, peanut butter, and brownies, are needed through the holidays for residents' parties and activities.[19]

As this list of sample needs is studied, it becomes clear that everyone could do something to demonstrate hospitality and compassion to the food insecure throughout the year.

Before I conclude this chapter, I want to share with you another category of the food insecure—the elderly. I recently read an article entitled "The Driver behind Meals on Wheels,"[20] which paints a word picture of Helen Barnes who, at the age of fifty-eight, helped found Meals on Wheels in 1971. At ninety she still drives two Meals on Wheels routes each week and arises each Monday morning at 4:30 a.m. to bake coffee cakes and assorted treats for the more than fifty Meals on Wheels volunteers. As the article suggests, more than 65 percent of their clients live alone, and the volunteer may well be the only person a client sees all day. Using the Meals on Wheels concept is a perfect way for believers to apply Matthew 25:40 by providing both spiritual and physical sustenance to those who are experiencing *food insecurity*.

A Concluding Consideration

Each Christmas when I place my "Cup of Christmas Tea" tea set on the tea cart and position beside it my copy of *A Cup of Christmas Tea* and *A Memory of Christmas Tea* I am reminded of the relationship between hospitality and compassion. *A Cup of Christmas Tea* describes how a nephew's reluctant visit to share a cup of tea with his elderly great-aunt becomes a source of joy and encouragement to aunt and nephew alike.[21] *A Memory of Christmas Tea* recounts the legacy the aunt passed on to her nephew to share a cup of Christmas tea with someone and, in essence, to extend compassion.[22] The lesson taught in each volume challenges me to expand my borders and extend compassion. May you too be prompted to practice compassionate hospitality so that others will see James 2:14–16 operative in your life.

Practicing Hospitality

1. Review both versions of the Compassionate Hospitality Equation.

   • Write your own compassionate hospitality equation.
   • Place it in a prominent place that will challenge you to put the equation into action.
   • Evaluate each time you extend hospitality against your equation by writing down what was successful and what you will change the next time you practice.

2. Read about some of the women recorded in the Bible who chose to extend compassion. Create a chart following the example below, which allows you to personalize God's compassion instructions to you. I started it for you.

God's Compassion Instructions

	Action	Ways I Could Practice This Instruction
Pharaoh's daughter Exodus 2:6–10	Chose to nurture baby Moses.	• Volunteer at the local crisis pregnancy center. • Investigate short- or long-term foster care.
The Hebrew midwives Shiphrah and Puah Exodus 1		
Ruth Ruth 1–4		
Mephibosheth's nurse 2 Samuel 4		
The widow of Zarephath 1 Kings 17:17–24		
The Jewish maid 2 Kings 5:1–5, 14–15		
The women at the tomb Matthew 28		
Elizabeth Luke 1:39–45		
The women following Jesus Luke 8		
Dorcas Acts 9:36–42		

3. Study the lives of some of the widows recorded in Scripture—Naomi (Ruth 1–4), the widow of Zarephath (1 Kings 17:7–24), the widow who knew how to handle money (Mark 12:41–44), Anna (Luke 2:22–27a), and Dorcas (Acts 9:36–42). Keeping the requirements of a true widow described in 1 Timothy 5:3–16 in focus, create a chart like the example below.

God's Requirements for His Widows

The requirements for widows found in 1 Timothy 5:3–16 are:

- to fix one's hope upon God (5:5)
-

Widow	Lifestyle Qualities	Ways I Can Use Her Life as an Example so That I Will Be Considered a True Widow
Naomi Ruth 1–4	Cultivated a positive relationship with her daughters-in-law so that they might desire to leave their native land in order to stay with her (Ruth 1:10).	Cultivate interpersonal relationships with younger women (Titus 2:3–5).
The widow of Zarephath 1 Kings 17:7–24		
The widow who knew how to handle money Mark 12:41–44		
Anna Luke 2:22–27a		
Dorcas Acts 9:36–42		

I will minister to the widows that I know by:
- intentionally developing quality relationships with them.
-

4. Develop a list of resources that will provide you with the knowledge you need to develop menus for individuals with dietary challenges and food allergies.

5. Provide consolation and comfort in both deed and word. Often it is easier for us to perform a deed than to provide words of comfort. Complete the "Comfort and Consolation Chart" to help you balance deed and word. Use the Scriptures provided as a starting point and then add your own.

Deed and Word Comfort and Consolation Chart

Scripture	Words I Might Speak	Deeds I Might Perform
John 14:16–18 • Someone called alongside to help.	"I am here to help. Please call me if there is something that you need."	Provide a meal for a grieving family.
2 Corinthians 1:3–7		
2 Corinthians 7:6		
1 Thessalonians 5:11		
2 Thessalonians 2:16–17		

Recipe Resources

A portion of this chapter talked about meeting the needs of family, guests, or those to whom you provide "portable hospitality" who have dietary constraints. Expose your family to the variety of diets described in Table 6.1 by using the recipes below to prepare the suggested menus.

LOW FAT MENU
Chicken Cacciatore

1 can (15-ounce) no-salt tomatoes in juice, cut up and drained
1 cup no-salt tomato sauce
1½ teaspoons crushed dried oregano

½ teaspoon crushed dried basil
1 tablespoon honey (optional)
¼ teaspoon white pepper (optional)
¼ cup fat-free chicken broth
3 cloves garlic, chopped
1 cup chopped onion
1 large green pepper, cut in 1-inch strips
¾ pound skinless chicken breast meat, cut into 2-inch
     cubes
¾ cup frozen green peas
1 tablespoon balsamic vinegar

Place cut-up canned tomatoes that have been thoroughly drained, tomato sauce, oregano, basil, honey, and pepper in a 2–3-quart saucepan. Cover and simmer 15 minutes.

Heat 4 tablespoons broth in a large skillet over medium high heat. Stir-fry garlic, onion, green pepper, and chicken for about 10 minutes, until chicken is no longer pink inside. Add chicken, onion, and green pepper to sauce and simmer, partially covered, 10 minutes. Add peas and balsamic vinegar, and cook uncovered an additional 5 minutes.

Serves 4

Angel Food Cake with Fruit Glaze

Fruit Glaze:
1 1-pound package frozen whole strawberries
5–6 teaspoons granulated sugar
5–6 tablespoons water

Thaw frozen strawberries in a bowl, covered, overnight in the refrigerator. Spoon sugar and water onto strawberries and let stand until time to serve. Stir occasionally throughout the day and before serving over dessert. Keep chilled until ready to use.

Angel Food Cake

1½ cups powdered sugar
1 cup cake flour
1½ cups egg whites (about 12)
1½ teaspoons cream of tartar
1 cup granulated sugar
1½ teaspoons vanilla
½ teaspoon almond extract
¼ teaspoon salt

Heat oven to 375 degrees. Mix powdered sugar and flour. Beat egg whites and cream of tartar in 3-quart bowl on medium speed until foamy. Beat in granulated sugar on high speed, 2 tablespoons at a time, adding vanilla, almond extract, and salt with the last addition of sugar; continue beating until stiff and glossy. Do not under-beat.

Sprinkle sugar-flour mixture, ¼ cup at a time, over meringue, folding in just until sugar-flour mixture disappears. Spread batter in ungreased tube pan (10 x 4 inches). Cut gently through batter with metal spatula. Bake until cracks feel dry and top springs back when touched lightly, 30 to 35 minutes.

Invert pan on heatproof funnel; let hang until cake is cool. Remove from pan. Spread top of cake with Fruit Glaze if desired.

16 servings; 130 calories per serving

Chocolate Angel Food Cake: Substitute ¼ cup cocoa for ¼ cup of the flour. Omit almond extract.

Coconut Angel Food Cake: Fold in 1 cup shredded coconut, ½ cup at a time, after folding in sugar-flour mixture.

Crock-Pot Beef Chili with Non-fat Cheese

½ pound dried pinto or kidney beans
2 cans whole tomatoes (28 ounces each)
2 medium onions, coarsely chopped
2 cloves garlic, crushed
½ cup finely chopped parsley
2 pounds lean ground beef
2–3 tablespoons chili powder (add to taste)
Salt (add to taste)
1 teaspoon pepper
1 teaspoon cumin seed (optional)

Wash beans; place in bowl and add water until about 2 inches above beans. Soak overnight. Simmer until softened. Drain and place in Crock-Pot. Add to beans: tomatoes, onions, garlic, and parsley.

In a large skillet, sauté the beef for about 15 minutes to remove excess fat. Drain and add meat to other ingredients in the Crock-Pot. Season with chili powder, salt, pepper, and cumin seed; mix thoroughly. Cover and cook on low setting for 8 to 14 hours or on high for 4 to 5½ hours.

One hour before serving, taste for seasoning and add additional chili powder if necessary. (Note: If cooked on high setting, beans do not need to be soaked or precooked.)

Serves 12

Cornbread Muffins with Honey

1 cup all-purpose flour
¾ cup cornmeal
2–4 tablespoons sugar (optional)
1 tablespoon double-acting baking powder
1 teaspoon salt
1 egg
⅔ cup milk
⅓ cup butter (or margarine), melted, or olive oil

Preheat oven to 425 degrees. Grease twelve 2½-inch muffin-pan cups.

In medium bowl with fork, mix together flour, cornmeal, sugar, baking powder, and salt.

In a small bowl with fork, beat together egg, milk, and butter (or margarine) and pour egg mixture into flour mixture all at once. Stir until flour is moistened and quickly spoon into muffin pan. Bake about 20 minutes.

(Note: For 8 x 8 baking pan, grease pan. Prepare batter as above and pour into prepared pan. Spread evenly and bake 25 minutes or until golden.)

Serves 12

Orange-Baked Apples

6 small baking apples
½ cup unsweetened apple juice
1 cup water
1 teaspoon cinnamon
1 small orange, sliced
2 tablespoons sugar (or 2 packets Equal)

185

Preheat oven to 350 degrees. Core apples and remove ¼ of top peel. Place apples in shallow baking pan. Combine water, juice, and cinnamon. Pour over apples. Arrange orange slices around apples to help flavor liquid. Cover pan with aluminum foil and bake about 30–35 minutes or until fork-tender. Remove from oven and sprinkle with sugar (or Equal).

Serves 6

VEGETARIAN MENU
Greek Village Salad

4 or 5 medium tomatoes, cut in wedges
1 medium cucumber, sliced diagonally
1 small green pepper, thinly sliced
5 green onions, sliced
5 radishes, sliced
½ small head Romaine lettuce
2 tablespoons chopped fresh dill or 2 teaspoons
     dill weed
15 green or black marinated Greek olives
Salt and black pepper to taste

Dressing:
½ cup olive oil
¼ cup vinegar
1 large garlic clove, minced
2 tablespoons chopped fresh parsley
pinch of crushed dried leaf oregano
¼ pound Feta cheese, diced (about ½ cup)

Combine tomatoes, cucumber, green pepper, green onions, radishes, lettuce, dill, and olives in a large, shallow salad bowl. Stir or shake dressing ingredients to mix well. Pour over salad. Toss gently but thoroughly. Garnish with Feta cheese.

Makes 6 to 8 servings

Vegetarian Lentils, Pasta & Rice

¼ cup olive oil
1 large onion, chopped
2 garlic cloves, minced
1 cup lentils, rinsed
1 (8-ounce) can tomato sauce
4 cups chicken broth or water
2 cups cooked elbow or tube macaroni
2 cups cooked long grain rice
salt and pepper to taste
1 tablespoon chopped fresh parsley
lemon wedges for garnish

Heat olive oil in a large saucepan. Add onion and garlic. Sauté until onion is tender. Add lentils. Sauté 1 minute. Stir in tomato sauce. Cook 1 minute to blend flavors. Add broth or water. Bring to a boil. Reduce heat and cover. Cook over medium-low heat 40 minutes or until lentils are tender. Fold in cooked macaroni, rice, salt, and pepper. Heat through, stirring frequently. Garnish with parsley and lemon wedges.

Makes 6 to 8 servings

Creamy Pudding with Berries

⅓ cup sugar
2 tablespoons cornstarch
⅛ teaspoon salt
2 cups of milk
¼ cup unfiltered apple juice
2 egg yolks, lightly beaten
2 tablespoons butter or margarine
1 teaspoon vanilla
assorted fruit (berries work great)

In a 2-quart pan, stir together sugar, cornstarch, and salt. Gradually add milk and apple juice until blended. Set mixture over medium heat and cook, stirring constantly, until it boils; boil for 1 minute. Remove from heat. Stir part of the hot sauce into beaten yolks, and then return all to pan and cook for 30 seconds. Remove from heat. Stir in butter and vanilla until butter is melted.

Layer spoonfuls of pudding and fruit in 4 stemmed glasses. If you use nectarines, be sure to end top layer with pudding so fruit will not darken. Chill until ready to serve.

Makes 4 servings

SEMI-VEGETARIAN MENU
Vegetable Combo Pizza

Pizza Dough:
1 cup plus 2 tablespoons water
2 tablespoons olive or vegetable oil
3 cups flour
1 teaspoon sugar (optional)
1 teaspoon salt
2½ teaspoons regular or quick-acting active dry yeast

Place all ingredients in bread pan in the order listed. Select WHITE DOUGH cycle.

Move oven rack to lowest position. Heat oven to 400 degrees. Grease 2 cookie sheets. Divide dough in half. Pat each half into 12-inch circle on cookie sheet with floured fingers. Spread with favorite toppings. Bake 18–20 minutes or until crust is light brown.

Makes 2 pizza crusts

Herb-Cheese Pizza Crust:
Add 2 tablespoons grated Parmesan cheese and 1½ teaspoons dried basil, oregano, thyme, or Italian seasonings
to the flour.

Vegetable Pizza Toppings:
tomato sauce
Italian seasonings
mozzarella (grated)
Parmesan cheese
sliced vegetables (tomatoes, zucchini, mushrooms,
       pineapple)

Season tomato sauce with Italian seasonings and spread
mixture onto pizza crust. Top with mozzarella, parmesan
cheese, and sliced vegetables.

Spinach Salad

1 pound spinach, torn into bite-size pieces (about 8 cups)
4 ounces mushrooms, sliced (about 1½ cups)
1 cup bean sprouts
6 ounces water chestnuts
6 red onion slices
5 hard-boiled eggs, sliced

Toss all ingredients. Serve with Italian dressing.

Makes 6 servings

Pineapple Ice

6 ounces fresh pineapple (or canned)
3 tablespoons honey
1 to 1¼ trays ice cubes

Cut the pineapple into chunks; put in the blender container with the honey and blend until it is a thick liquid. Taste for more honey. Add a few ice cubes and blend at high speed until half crushed. Keep adding cubes until the mixture is very thick.

Makes 4 servings

Strawberry Ice

Follow the recipe for Pineapple Ice using an 18-ounce package of frozen strawberries.

DIABETIC MENU
Fruit Salad

1 cup water-packed pineapple chunks or tidbits
1 cup fresh orange slices
1 cup diced, unpeeled apple
1 cup canned, unsweetened drained cherries
1 cup plain, unsweetened low-fat yogurt

Combine pineapple, orange slices, apple, and cherries in a medium bowl. Gently fold in yogurt. Cover and refrigerate until thoroughly chilled.

Chicken Nut Stir-Fry

2 teaspoons peanut oil
2 stalks celery, chopped
2 carrots, peeled and diagonally sliced
1½ pounds skinless, boneless chicken breast halves, cut
        into strips
1 tablespoon cornstarch
¾ cup orange juice

3 tablespoons light soy sauce
1 tablespoon honey
1 teaspoon minced ginger
¼ cup cashews
¼ cup minced green onions

Heat 1 teaspoon of the oil in a wok over high heat. Add the carrots and celery and stir-fry for 3 minutes. Add remaining 1 teaspoon oil, then add the chicken, and stir-fry for 5 more minutes. In a small bowl, dissolve the cornstarch into the orange juice. Mix in the soy sauce, honey, and ginger. Add this sauce to the wok and cook over medium heat until thickened. Top with the cashews and green onions.

Makes 6 servings

Macaroni and Cheese

3 cups uncooked macaroni
¾ cup nonfat cottage cheese
1 egg white
¾ packet artificial sweetener
¼ cup and 2 tablespoons reduced-fat cheese, cubed
¼ cup and 2 tablespoons low-fat buttermilk
½ teaspoon liquid smoke flavoring
¾ cup crushed saltine crackers

Cook pasta in a large pot of boiling salted water until al dente. Grease a 2-quart casserole dish. In a food processor, blend cottage cheese until smooth. In a large bowl, combine cottage cheese, egg white, sweetener, cheese cubes, buttermilk, and liquid smoke until well mixed. Stir in pasta. Pour into prepared dish. Top with crushed crackers. Bake at 400 degrees for 30 minutes.

Makes 6 servings

Warm Apple Cinnamon Cobbler

4 apples peeled, cored, and sliced
1 cup water
2 teaspoons ground cinnamon
2 tablespoons cornstarch
¼ cup fructose (fruit sugar)
1 cup whole wheat pastry flour
1 teaspoon baking powder
¼ cup oil
½ cup low-fat buttermilk

Preheat oven to 375 degrees. In a large saucepan over medium heat, combine the apples, water, cinnamon, cornstarch, and fructose. Cook until apples are soft and mixture is thickened, about 10 minutes. Pour the apple mixture into the casserole dish.

Prepare biscuit dough by combining the whole wheat pastry flour and baking powder. Add the oil and stir until well mixed. Add the buttermilk; stir with a fork until flour mixture is moist. Add additional milk if necessary.

Drop biscuit dough by tablespoons on top of apples. Bake for 20 minutes or until biscuits are golden brown. Serve warm.

Makes 6 servings

French Onion Soup

6 beef bouillon cubes
5 cups boiling water
½ cup pure tomato juice
2 cups fresh onion rings
6 small unsalted Melba toast rounds
12 tablespoons grated Parmesan cheese

Dissolve bouillon cubes in boiling water. Add the tomato juice and onions. Cover and simmer gently for 25–30 minutes. Serve in warmed bowls with a Melba toast round. Sprinkle 2 tablespoons of Parmesan cheese on top of each.

Makes 6 servings

Poached Beef Tenderloin

2-pound beef tenderloin roast
1 tablespoon oil
4 cups water
1 10¾-ounce can reduced-sodium beef broth
1 cup red grape juice
2 cloves garlic, minced
1 teaspoon diced marjoram leaves
4 black peppercorns
3 whole cloves

Tie the beef roast with heavy string at 2-inch intervals. Brown the beef roast in oil over medium-high heat until all sides are browned. Pour off the drippings. Add the water, beef broth, grape juice, garlic, marjoram, peppercorns, and cloves. Bring to a boil, reduce the heat to medium-low; cover and simmer for 10 minutes per pound. The temperature should register 130 degrees. Do not overcook.

Remove the roast to a serving platter. Cover tightly with plastic wrap or aluminum foil and allow the roast to stand for 10 minutes before carving. The roast temperature will rise approximately 10 degrees to 140 degrees for rare. Remove the string and carve the roast into thin slices. Serve with steamed vegetables.

Makes 8 servings

Stuffed Artichokes with Carrots

artichokes (1 per person)
bread crumbs
butter

Cut off tip of artichoke leaves. Open flower and fill with bread crumbs. Place in a casserole dish with 1–2 inches of water. Place ½ tablespoon butter over each artichoke. Bake at 350 degrees for one hour or until tender.

7

Hospitality and CULTURE

For though I am free from all, I have made myself a servant to all, that I might win more of them.... I do it all for the sake of the gospel, that I may share with them in its blessings.

—1 CORINTHIANS 9:19, 23

o you enjoy traveling, meeting people, or eating new foods? I do! I think it is because I traveled extensively as a young girl. My father was in the U.S. Navy, and later in life he became a pastor of a church overseas. We lived in various places around the United States as well as in Japan and Australia. While the constant moving was not always easy—I lived in twenty-one different places by the time I was eighteen years old—I look back now and see the benefits of being exposed to the various cultures. I have wonderful memories of interesting people and places from all over the world.

My earliest memories as a young girl are from the beautiful country of Japan. I remember the people as courteous, hospitable, and generous gift-givers. I recall Japanese food introducing me to many new tastes and types, including various types of sea fish, squid, and seaweed cookies. I still enjoy eating the noodles I ate in Japan and have introduced them to my own children. I can clearly visualize the beautifully kept, serene gardens. I vividly recall the countless temples for and statues depicting their various gods. I remember the people-packed subway system and riding with my family on the "bullet trains." All of my memories are small puzzle pieces that create a picture of the Japanese culture.

Regardless of where I traveled with my family, the people were usually different from me in appearance, mannerisms, and beliefs. The geography and architecture exposed me to a variety of climates and historical events. The food was always interesting and creative by American norms! Each country had unique behavior characteristics, belief systems, and values making it a distinct culture.

Culture Impacts Hospitality

"To the weak I became weak, that I might win the weak. I have become all things to all people, that by all means I might save some" (1 Cor. 9:22). Why is it important to talk about culture in the context of hospitality? Culture impacts hospitality because, as noted in chapter 2, we cannot ignore the priority Scripture places on being hospitable to the stranger or alien (Ex. 22:21; Lev. 19:34; Deut. 10:12–21; Ps. 146:9; Heb. 12:2). You will recall the term *stranger* refers to an alien or foreigner. If hospitality to foreigners is a priority reflected throughout Scripture, we must each ask ourselves, "How can I be hospitable to strangers in my own country?"

We know that hospitality is a practical way to love people and ultimately share God's love for them. However, hospitality can be expressed very differently in various cultures. For this reason, understanding culture becomes a necessary tool for successfully practicing hospitality with foreigners or strangers.

Even if you do not travel abroad or participate in international missions, you will probably be confronted with different cultures within your own borders. The nations of the world have come to America. Its cities are filled with immigrants, students, and those who are here for business purposes. Think about your own community for a moment. What are the various cultures represented? In my own community I interact with several cultures—Asian, Hispanic, Middle Eastern, and Russian. I interact with diverse cultures each day as I fulfill my routine responsibilities of being a homemaker and mother. I also have had the privilege of teaching several international students representing the countries of Australia, Japan, Kenya, South Africa, and Spain. I do not have to travel outside my community to interact with internationals or, as Scripture calls them, *aliens* or *foreigners*. Acknowledging the unique culture each individual represents helps me to be more successful at extending hospitality in a meaningful way. Being hospitable allows forming relationships that hopefully will provide me with an opportunity to share the gospel.

Paul's Example of Culture

Paul addresses this idea of considering other people in the context of their cultures when he says, "I have become all things to all people, that by all means I might save some" (1 Cor. 9:22). He then gives specific examples of cross-cultural ministry, naming the Jews and Gentiles (1 Cor. 9:20–22). "To the Jews I became as a Jew" (1 Cor. 9:20), he said. Paul did not compromise his Christian faith while crossing cultures; he considered culture "within the limits of God's Word and his Christian conscience; he would be as culturally and socially Jewish as necessary when witnessing to Jews"[1] (see also Acts 16:3; 21:23–26; Rom. 9:3; 10:1; 11:14).

Paul was also willing to cross cultures by adapting his methods of communication to fit his audience. This is evident when Paul says, "To the weak I became weak" (1 Cor. 9:22). He was not referring to their physical condition but, rather, to those who were "weak in faith"[2] (Rom. 14:1–2; 15:1; 2 Cor. 11:29). Paul communicated simply for the benefit of his spiritually immature audience. We can learn much from Paul's example—primarily that we should attempt to understand and cross cultural barriers for *the sake of the gospel*. This motivation helps us understand culture in the context of hospitality so that we might have the opportunity to see people from all the nations of the world come to know Jesus Christ as their Lord and Savior (Acts 10:34–35). Let's define culture and then look at how understanding cultural differences can impact our practice of hospitality.

What Is Culture?

"So, whether you eat or drink, or whatever you do, do all to the glory of God. Give no offense to Jews or to Greeks or to the church of God, just as I try to please everyone in everything I do, not seeking my own advantage, but that of many, that they may be saved" (1 Cor. 10:31–33). Culture embraces everything that is influential in someone's life; culture is not merely differences in language and residential location. Consider how these definitions will affect your relationships with your foreign or cross-cultural guests. Culture is seen in numerous ways, including manners, customs, beliefs, religion, values, morals, language, government systems, work ethics, family structure, and interpersonal relationships.

Our survey participants provided several helpful examples illustrating how cultural differences are seen in daily living. Melitsa Barnes writes, "Cultural differences are seen in how people relate to each other." She adds that in other cultures it is often on a deeper level—relationships tend to go beyond a superficial level (people have fewer friends, but are often closer to the ones they have). Other differences include food items and what they signify or symbolize. Being aware of these traditions allows us to understand others better and, in turn, allows us to minister to them more effectively.

Sue Edwards tells us, "Middle Eastern people with Islamic backgrounds have meat and alcohol restrictions in their diets. Older people are extremely important in social gatherings. Being the oldest person brings great honor and must be recognized." Sue explains, "When foreign guests are in our home we try to incorporate as many of their traditions as possible, such as taking off shoes, making toasts, preparing different types of meals or ways of serving them."

Patti Morse shares, "We have experienced both ethical and dietary differences. Several of our foreign students have religious prohibitions against eating red meat and pork, among other things, and specific dietary preferences with each meal, such as rice, couscous. When sitting in a group, we must be careful not to cross our legs because this is an offense, as well." Patti explains that showing the sole of one's foot to another is an insult. Also, she says, "When visiting, we must always address the man, for to address the woman is a sign of disrespect for the head of the house. When hosting our family from Bulgaria, we had to remember not to nod our head in response to a question, for such a gesture is disrespectful in their culture. Many differences!" From Patti we learn that it is very important that we do everything possible not to offend those having different backgrounds while doing all we can to make them feel loved, accepted, and comfortable in our presence. This brings glory to God and opens the door for the gospel to be shared.

Lisa-Ann Chun observes that Americans often value their friends over family, while the Chinese culture places great value and respect on family members as most important of all.

If we do not understand cultural differences we probably will not understand others' values, beliefs, and behaviors. As well, we may be limited in effectively communicating our love and, most importantly, God's love. First Corinthians 10:32 reminds believers to be careful to "give no offense" because their ultimate goal in understanding culture is that others "might be saved."

At this point, some of you may be thinking—only missionaries need to consider culture; why discuss culture in a book on hospitality? However, if hospitality lovingly meets the needs of others, how can this goal be accomplished if we do not understand cultural differences? I would like to suggest that hospitality *is* missions. Hospitality is a tool you can use to love people and make "disciples of all nations" of the world (Matt. 28:18–20). Consideration of culture is a key element in practicing hospitality as you endeavor to model Christ's love—so "that they may be saved" (1 Cor. 10:33).

Culture and Hospitality

"She opens her hand to the poor and reaches out her hands to the needy" (Prov. 31:20). Now that we have defined culture generally, let's apply the concepts of culture specifically to practicing hospitality. The purpose of this section is not to give you a list of hospitality dos and don'ts for every country in the world—space does not permit that! You can, however, consider several key areas each time you entertain or interact with people from other cultures. In other words, these are areas where you can expect differences between American culture and the home culture of your guest. You may need to make inquiries or conduct your own research for the specific country of your guest (or host, if you are the guest in her home). As you anticipate differences in the cultures, you will be more likely to communicate effectively and experience less frustration as you open your home to culturally different guests. These guidelines can help regardless of the type of entertainment or the nationality of the guest:

- Learn how to pronounce the name of your guest correctly. Do not use an American version of the name or a nickname unless your guest specifically requests this.
- Remember that it takes time to build trust, to establish a friendship, and to develop understanding of people from another culture.
- Make an effort to learn about your guest's homeland— geography, government, climate, and history are good places to start. Check out books from your local library or use the Internet for resources.
- Understand the cultural differences in terms of how relational respect is communicated. Most guests from foreign countries will still have a high regard for authority, age, or position. In contrast, Americans tend to view everyone as their equal, which leads to a more informal approach to relationships. Your guest may be processing your friendship through the class system of his or her homeland. Behavior that seems reserved, quiet, or nonparticipatory may be appropriate because of the way relational respect is communicated in their culture. It does not necessarily mean they are not having an enjoyable time!

In addition to the general reminders above, there are several specific areas to consider when demonstrating hospitality to cross-cultural guests: time orientation, task/goal focus, etiquette, and food. You can anticipate differences in how you and your guest will each view these areas.

Time Orientation

There are obvious differences in time orientation among industrialized countries (e.g., United States, Canada, or Britain) and developing countries (e.g., Latin American or African countries). The American preoccupation with time can be seen in how many wear watches, carry Palm Pilots, and are impatient for any length of wait. They make appointments well in advance for each event, write agendas for every gathering, and practice management strategies that will maximize their time use. In general, hospitality events are determined by Western cultural views on time. However, many other countries in the world are not concerned about the time at all. International Students Incorporated explains it this way:

> In some countries, the clock does not carry the same importance as it does in the United States. Your friend may not come from a time-controlled culture. In some nations, for instance, it is considered proper to arrive an hour or more late to an event. In other cultures, an invitation must be extended several times before it is accepted.[3]

It is easy to see why it is important to consider differences in your views on time when entertaining cross-cultural guests. If you send out invitations, your guests may not realize the need to respond to you. Expect to follow up with a phone call or another method to confirm attendance. Remember that invitations are rarely used in other countries.

Another way to adapt is to plan on having guests show up who did not RSVP. Prepare enough food for everyone on your invitation list. For example, if you invited twenty-five but have only heard from ten, still plan on preparing food for twenty-five. You can always freeze or give away leftover food.

You can also expect your guests to be late. It is very acceptable in many parts of the world to be up to an hour late. Not only is it acceptable, it is a common practice. Your international guest may not know that being late is considered poor manners in America. Prepare a meal that will not be ruined if your guests are late, for example, soup. Another strategy is to plan on serving your meal much later than the invitation time. If your guests are invited for 6:00 p.m., plan on serving dinner at 7:00 p.m. Have beverages and hors d'oeuvres available to tide over hungry guests, allowing others extra time to arrive before serving the main meal.

Finally, don't be surprised if your foreign guests stay longer than your American guests normally do. Staying very late into the night is acceptable in many countries. Remember, the clock does not rule in many other cultures!

Task/Goal Focus

Americans are notorious for their drive to complete a task and accomplish their goals. This is often reflected in hospitality by placing the emphasis on *the process* rather than on *the people*. Yes, you need to plan and be organized so you are prepared for your event. However, don't forget that you practice good management strategies so you are free to focus on the real priority—the people! When you entertain, it is very easy to miss the people for the plan. You can spend the whole evening watching the clock, keeping the kitchen cleaned up, and providing entertainment rather than simply enjoying the company of your guests in a leisurely manner. Most guests will place a higher value on meaningful conversation than on a nicely prepared meal.

One way to help keep people as the priority, rather than the plan, is never to leave a guest alone so that you can complete a task. If you need to leave the room to finish meal preparations or for another reason, make sure your husband or children remain with the guest, serving as the host or hostess in your absence.

Another way to keep people first is to focus on having meaningful conversation rather than on serving a successful meal. Make a list of questions that will stimulate your conversation. Remember, however, many cross-cultural guests will not be accustomed to talking while eating; for many it is considered impolite. You may find that meaningful conversations will occur before and after the meal.

Keep people first by waiting to clean up the dishes, kitchen, and other supplies until after your guests leave. Do only the minimum required to prevent food from spoiling. This will keep you with your guests. Your guests will return home and your cleaning will wait for you.

Another people-first tip is to be flexible! Think ahead and create a list of ideas for activities to do with your guest. Consider playing games, looking at family photos, or taking a walk. However, don't be disappointed if you don't do anything on your list. The most meaningful part of being together will probably be when you simply take the time to listen and talk to your friends.

Etiquette

Another significant difference when extending hospitality to people from other countries will be what is considered acceptable in terms of manners or etiquette. Three key areas are gift-giving, table etiquette, and conversation.

Gift-giving

Each country has specific rules governing gift-giving practices; however, a few general guidelines typically always apply. First, *hostess gifts* are important. While proper American etiquette still suggests bringing a hostess gift, it is rarely practiced in our society. However, gift-giving in most parts of the world is *very* important. It is very offensive if you do not take a gift for your host or hostess. Therefore, always be prepared to take an appropriate gift; likewise, be prepared to receive a gift graciously.

Gifts should be *moderate in size*. You neither want to flaunt wealth or offend by stinginess. Also, give unique gifts. When you have multiple guests or hosts, give each person a unique gift. Only members of the same group should receive the same type of gift. Giving students the same gift would be acceptable but the instructor ought to receive something different. Most countries have a great respect for authority or position, and their citizens will be offended if rank or class is not considered in the gift-giving.

Also consider the *color* of your gift. Americans rarely find colors culturally unacceptable; however, citizens of many other countries do. In China, "white, blue, or black gifts are associated with funerals, whereas red, pink, and yellow are 'joyful' colors; yet don't use red ink, because a message written in red ink implies the severing of a relationship."[4] In addition to considering the color of your gift, there may be other cultural *symbols* to avoid. You will need to investigate the symbols to avoid for each country.

Consider the *timing* for opening the gift. Etiquette rules apply here as well. Americans find it acceptable to open the gift in front of the giver. However, many countries consider this very offensive. If you are unsure, check with your guest about how you can reflect a grateful acceptance. Simply ask, "If I were in your country, would I open the gift now or wait?"

Avoid gifts with company logos on them. This can appear self-serving. Flowers or candy such as a box of chocolates is generally an appropriate gift in any country. However, take the time to check on the kind and number appropriate to bring. Flowers are often symbolic, and the number of flowers is often tied to superstitions related to good and evil. You can easily offend your guests or hosts by not considering symbolic meanings in their countries. In most countries, including Austria, Germany, and the Czech Republic,[5] you will want to avoid red roses since they are reserved for romantic love. Also, some flowers are associated with death, like chrysanthemums in Belgium.[6]

Items from your home state also make suitable gifts for almost any occasion and for citizens of any country. Historical or factual books about your state or its home-grown products such as honey, syrups, or teas make wonderful gifts for cross-cultural guests or hosts.

Table Etiquette

Remind yourself that you have established table etiquette out of courtesy and respect for others. You want to make each meal a pleasant and enjoyable experience for all who are seated at the table. However, American guidelines are not necessarily what communicate courtesy and respect to someone from another country. Consider differences in acceptable etiquette out of a desire to make your guest feel welcome and at home. Remember, etiquette guidelines are not moral absolutes. It does not matter how you hold your silverware or serve the meal in light of eternity! What does matter is that you have demonstrated sincere love to your guest.

Expect your cross-cultural friend to be unfamiliar with basic American table etiquette guidelines such as waiting to eat until the hostess begins and placing napkins in the lap. Requiring strict etiquette will make your event uncomfortable and potentially embarrassing to those who are unfamiliar with the rules of etiquette. Take a very informal approach to any event with international guests attending. Building a relationship is the first priority, not teaching etiquette. Once the relationships are built you may have an opportunity to share American customs related to etiquette or manners.

Take the time to explain your table setting. Explain what fork to use with what course, which beverage glass belongs to whom, where to locate the bread plate, or the use of the condiments on the table. This helps your guest to feel comfortable throughout the meal.

Fingers are often more acceptable to use than forks and knives in some countries and, therefore, your guest may not be comfortable using silverware initially. Be sure your guest knows what utensil should be used if your place setting has more than one fork or spoon. Burping while eating is often a way to affirm the meal has been satisfying and tasteful in many countries such as some in Asia. Americans generally "clean their plate" and then place their silverware across the plate to indicate they are finished. However, in many countries, if you clean your plate it means you have not had enough and the hostess will continue to fill your plate. Your international guests may leave food on their plates to indicate they have had enough. It does not necessarily mean they didn't like the food. Also, expect to offer food or refreshments more than one time. In many countries it is considered impolite to accept on the first invitation. Offer two or three times to ensure your guest is not just being polite by refusing refreshments.[7]

If you have children, discuss with them in advance that your guests may do things differently. Encourage them to model the appropriate behavior that is expected from your family. Your children can be key participants in making your cross-cultural guests feel welcome because of their unpretentious acceptance of those who are different from themselves. Finally, praying before a meal may be an unfamiliar practice to your guests, so before praying simply say, "It is our practice or custom to pray and thank God for our food before we eat."

Conversation

Good communication is the goal for establishing conversation guidelines. You want to maximize every opportunity to build your relationship. Guidelines for communication prepared by International Students Incorporated[8] are very helpful to remember:

- *Listen attentively.* By listening carefully to what your guest is saying, you are paying her a high compliment and expressing your genuine interest and concern.
- *Speak carefully to be understood.* Remember that your friend may not fully understand what you are saying. Articulate your words and speak clearly.
- *Avoid idioms or slang.* Your English may be quite different from the classroom English your guest learned in his or her homeland.
- *Use jokes or humor sparingly.* Lacking the American cultural context and immersion in the English language, cross-cultural guests may have difficulty understanding jokes or humor.
- *Explain words and phrases patiently.* Invite your friend to ask you about words or phrases she does not understand.
- *Respect differences of opinion.* It's important to share what you think—honestly, but with sensitivity—and to reflect that you respect your guest's ideas and opinions.

In addition to these suggestions, expect to lead the conversation. You will need to initiate most of the conversation throughout the course of your event. Some countries consider it bad manners to talk at all during a meal. What Americans interpret as rude silence may actually be polite table manners. I read a pamphlet entitled *Foreign Missions in Your Own Backyard*[9] to help me create a list of conversation topics; perhaps my list will help you generate your own list of ideas. Review the list before your guest arrives so you are prepared to facilitate meaningful conversation. By asking intentional questions you will discover more about your guest each time you interact with him or her. Below are a few sample questions to get you started.

Food

- What types of food are popular in your culture?
- Do families eat together?
- What times of day are meals served?
- What is your favorite American food?

Clothing

- What types of clothing do people in your culture wear at work, home, or for special occasions?
- Is traditional clothing still worn and if so, when?
- Are there special symbolic colors for clothing?

Housing

- How would you describe a typical home in your country?

Children and Education

- How do parents select names for their children?
- When do children start school?
- What is the educational system like?
- What are the differences between schools in your country and in the United States?

Leisure Activities/Sports

- What sports are popular in your homeland?
- What do you like to do with your free time?
- Do you follow any American sports?

Spirituality

- What is your understanding of religion in America?
- What is the national religion in your country?
- Who is God?

Holidays and Special Occasions

- What are the major national holidays in your country?
- What are the major religious holidays in your country?
- How do you celebrate birthdays or anniversaries?

Personal

- What do you miss most about your homeland?
- What has been your hardest adjustment to American culture?

Food

Food is probably one of the more obvious areas where differences exist. Food can represent differences in three areas—methods of preparation, types or kinds of food including the spices used, and service style. Below are some general guidelines for preparing food that your cross-cultural guest might enjoy.

Remember dietary restrictions due to religious, cultural, or individual preferences. Hindus and Buddhists are strict vegetarians. They eat no meat, fish, poultry, or eggs.[10] Likewise, Muslims and many Jews do not eat pork.[11] If you are unsure of your guest's diet restrictions, be sure to ask in advance so you can plan appropriately.

Limit the use of dairy products. Most cross-cultural guests will not be overly familiar with dairy products such as cheese and often do not like them. Asians and Africans, for example, eat very few dairy products.

Processed meats, such as deli meats or canned tuna, are generally not acceptable to most internationals. Use fresh meats when including meat in your menu. It is always better to rely on fresh foods. Foods that are simple, fresh, and prepared at home are more likely to be enjoyed by your guests. Remember: America has the unique distinction of being the land of the processed, fast, and frozen food! We are very comfortable with the appearance, texture, and taste of these types of foods. However, most other countries rely primarily on fresh foods.

Avoid casseroles or dishes with many chopped ingredients. Try to serve foods where the ingredients are identifiable so people unfamiliar with the food will know what they are eating. Most internationals will not enjoy casseroles. Chicken, fish, fruit, and vegetables are usually good choices to serve for most cross-cultural guests. Additionally, lamb and seafood are often eaten more frequently in other countries.

Fruit is often the preferred dessert. Simple fruit desserts or ice creams are usually preferred by most cross-cultural guests rather than very rich desserts[12] such as a seven-layer chocolate cake or coconut cream pie.

Take the time to explain to your guests the service style you have selected. Don't assume they will know how to proceed through a buffet line. Likewise, serving yourself and passing the dishes at the table is very American, and most will not have seen this service method before. Be sure to monitor that the dishes are being passed along and that everyone has been served each item.

When you entertain guests from other countries, you as the hostess and organizer of the event must anticipate these differences. As you do, you will be more likely to meet the genuine needs of your guests, communicate your love, and ultimately have an opportunity to demonstrate Christ's love for them.

Internationals in Our Backyard

"So Peter opened his mouth and said: 'Truly I understand that God shows no partiality, but in every nation anyone who fears him and does what is right is acceptable to him'" (Acts 10:34–35). Having defined culture and taken the time to examine how culture will impact your hospitality, you need to ask yourself the question: How can I practically apply what we have been discussing? Many of you are already involved in cross-cultural relationships and have your own experience from which to draw. My prayer is that you will continue to develop and deepen these relationships for the sake of the gospel (1 Cor. 9:19–23). For others however, *crossing cultures* is a new thought! You may not know where to begin. There is one simple way we can all be involved in cross-cultural relationships and never leave our homes, and that is by opening our home and sharing our families with international students.

Every year over "550,000 international students and visiting scholars from nearly every nation are in the United States—many with their families."[13] Students who are studying in the United States often return to their respective homelands to assume leadership positions in government, business, and education. In other words, international students are tomorrow's world leaders! Many countries closed to missionaries are sending students to study in the United States. Believers need to catch the vision for the world impact they can have by extending friendship and hospitality to international students. Most are eager to establish friendships with Americans. Unfortunately, the experts say that most international students will *never* enter an American home.[14] How sad to think even believers have failed to extend hospitality to them. I would urge you to consider extending hospitality to an international student.

If you do not know how to locate international students in your area, you can contact the international student advisor at the college or university nearest you. They often already have programs in which you can participate. You can also contact International Students Inc. (ISI) for assistance in locating students in your area. ISI is a national ministry organization that specializes in matching international students with caring believers. They work all over the United States.[15] They have a variety of helpful resources including *Country Profile Series*, *Religions Profile Series*, and many booklets on befriending and evangelizing international students.

A Concluding Consideration

For those of us who have children, there is one final area to consider: what are we modeling for our children? How do we encourage our children to be hospitable towards others who are culturally different? I know that as a mom I have many hopes and desires for my children. First, of course, is that someday they will choose to submit their hearts and lives to Jesus Christ as their personal Savior. However, I also pray that they will grow into men and women who are compassionate and who love people practically. I hope people take priority over possessions in their lives and that they learn to sacrifice personal comfort willingly in order to serve others. I long to see them grow into adults who are kind, considerate, and caring towards the needy. I desire for them to sincerely enjoy and love people who are culturally different. I pray that they will develop a passion to communicate God's love to others and demonstrate it through practical service. In other words—I hope they are hospitable! Biblically hospitable people are caring, self-sacrificing, and compassionate.

I often wonder, however, if I am modeling for my children the character attributes I desire to see in their lives. Am I exposing them to life experiences that will develop a heart of compassion for people who are culturally different? Am I filling their heads with spiritual knowledge but failing to help them know how to live out their faith through practical application, knowing that failure to do this will lead to arrogance and self-righteousness? In other words, do my children understand that meeting the needs of others is as important as managing their time, working hard, and accomplishing tasks?

In conclusion, I would like to suggest that teaching our children to be hospitable to people who are culturally different is critical toward developing the character attributes of compassion, kindness, and love. Hospitality can expose them to people with a variety of life circumstances and needs. It can cultivate empathy for other people. Jan Johnson, author of *Growing Compassionate Kids*, suggests that empathy is critical for our children to learn because "a child growing in empathy is moving from isolation to connection, from self-centeredness to others-awareness, from hostility to hospitality."[16] If we do not reach out across cultures, we will rob our children of valuable life lessons in loving people. We cannot afford to neglect hospitality if we desire to model for our children the depth of God's love for the nations of the world.

Practicing Hospitality

1. Reflect on God's heart for all the nations of the world. Scripture describes God as an impartial God; he loves and judges all people by his same righteous standards. Consider the impartiality and love of God towards all people by reviewing the following passages and writing a summary statement to remind you of the principles taught.

Scriptures dealing with the impartiality of God	What this passage tells me about God and his heart for the nations
2 Chronicles 19:7	
Matthew 5:43–48	
Matthew 28:16–20	
John 3:16	
Acts 10:34–35	
Acts 15:19–21	
Romans 2:5–11	
Romans 10:11–13	
Galatians 2:6	
Ephesians 2:8–9	

2. Introduce new cultures to your family. Learn about one new country and its culture each month:

- Select one country for each month of the year.
- Purchase a world atlas or world map and locate the country you have selected.
- Visit your local library to find books on the history, government, geography, and weather of the country.
- Pick up a copy of *Operation World: The Day-by-Day Guide to Praying for the World* by Patrick Johnstone.[17] Pray for your country each day. Review with your family the various demographics listed.
- E-mail or write a missionary who lives in that country for a realistic view of everyday life in your selected country.
- Research the food and prepare a traditional meal. If a whole meal is too much, prepare only dessert. See the recipe resources at the end of this chapter to get you started.
- Learn about national holidays, heroes, and heroines.
- Find pictures of the people and learn about their native costumes. When possible, have your children dress up.

- Learn a phrase or song in the language of the country you have selected. If a phrase is too much, simply learn to say "hello" in the native language.

3. Do you do all things for "the sake of the gospel" (1 Cor. 9:23)? Evaluate how you would respond to the cultural differences we discussed: time orientation, task/goal focus, etiquette, and food. Ask the Lord to mature you in patience, flexibility, and love towards others who are culturally different, for the sake of the gospel. There is a sample prayer in the first box; complete the others on your own.

Cultural Differences	Cultural differences in this area would be *challenging* for me personally because:	My prayer for God to grow my character in this area for the sake of the gospel:
Time Orientation		Dear Heavenly Father, forgive me for my intolerance toward others who do not view time as I do. Please help me to be patient, flexible, and loving toward others *for the sake of the gospel.*
Task/Goal Focus		*. . . for the sake of the gospel.*
Etiquette		*. . . for the sake of the gospel.*
Food		*. . . for the sake of the gospel.*

4. Do you know how to share your faith with someone from another religion? Take the time to develop answers for the following questions. Find three or four specific Scriptures to support each of your answers. Pray that the Lord will give you the opportunity to share your faith. Finally, consider memorizing several of the verses you have selected.

- How would you describe your God? What are his attributes?

    The attributes of my God are . . .

- How does your religion define sin?

    The Bible defines sin as . . .

- How does your religion view death? What happens when you die?

    When I die . . .

- Who is Jesus?

    Jesus is . . .

- What is the meaning or purpose of life?

    The purpose of my life is to . . .

5. Consider reaching out as a family to an international student. Make a list of routine family activities suitable for including an international student. Use the list below to get you started.

- Athletic events such as your children's sporting events, college games, or other family hobbies; for example, hiking.
- Family celebrations, birthday parties, or special family vacation days like trips to theme parks.
- Family day trips such as taking a picnic to the beach or to a national park.
- Holidays such as Thanksgiving, Christmas, and Easter, which provide a wonderful opportunity to share your faith as you explain the holiday celebrations.
- Shopping trips to local malls or grocery stores help students learn their way around the community and teach them where the best deals can be found.

217

Recipe Resources

A simple way to introduce international flavors to your family and friends is to host an "International Dessert Night." Use the dessert recipes below to get started and then create your own international menus for future events.

International Dessert Menu

Australia: Pavlova (Meringue Dessert; also popular in
     New Zealand)
Brazil: Brasileiras (Brazilian Coconut Cookies)
France: Mousse au Chocolat (Chocolate Mousse)
Spain: Flan (Caramel Custard)

Australia: *Pavlova*
Meringue Dessert

5 egg whites
10 ounces caster sugar
½ teaspoon vanilla essence
1 teaspoon vinegar
3 dessertspoons cold water
whipped cream
fruit—kiwi, fruit salad, bananas, strawberries, etc.

Place egg whites in mixer; begin mixing till frothy. Add all other ingredients. Beat until quite stiff (on highest speed). Spread mixture on an aluminum-covered, round pizza pan sprinkled with cornstarch. Form into a circle. Bake at 300 degrees for 20 minutes then at 250 degrees for 1 hour and 10 minutes. Cool slowly, not opening oven till cold. Decorate with whipped cream, fresh and/or canned fruit. Chill.

Serves 10

Brazil: *Brasileiras*
Coconut Cookies

1 cup granulated sugar
½ cup water
4 egg yolks, slightly beaten
¼ cup all-purpose flour
2¼ cups freshly grated coconut or packaged coconut
½ teaspoon vanilla

In heavy saucepan, combine sugar and water. Cook over moderate heat, stirring until sugar dissolves. Cook syrup undisturbed until candy thermometer reads 230 degrees. (A small amount of syrup dropped into ice water should immediately form a hard thread.)

In small mixer bowl, combine egg yolks and flour until well blended. Add 2 tablespoons of the hot syrup, stirring constantly. Slowly add this mixture to the syrup remaining in the pan, stirring constantly. Add coconut and simmer over low heat, stirring constantly, until mixture becomes thick. (Do not let it boil.) Remove from heat and quickly stir in vanilla.

Let mixture cool to room temperature.

Preheat oven to 375 degrees. Shape cookie dough into small balls. Arrange balls 1 inch apart on lightly greased baking sheets. Bake 15 minutes or until cookies are a delicate golden brown. Remove to wire racks to cool.

Makes about 3 dozen

France: *Mousse au Chocolat*
Chocolate Mousse

¼ pound semisweet chocolate, broken into chunks

4 egg yolks
4 tablespoons butter, softened
4 egg whites
½ cup heavy cream
chocolate curls

Melt chocolate in the top of a double boiler over barely simmering water. In small bowl of electric mixer, beat egg yolks until thick and lemon-colored (about 10 minutes). Add butter a tablespoon at a time to chocolate, beating until mixture is smooth. Add the beaten egg yolks and cook, beating constantly, until the mixture has thickened and is smooth, about 5 minutes. (Do not let mixture come to a boil.) Remove pan from the heat. Set top portion of double boiler aside and cool chocolate mixture to room temperature, about 30 minutes.

In large mixer bowl with clean beaters, beat egg whites until soft peaks form. Gently fold chocolate mixture into egg whites, folding until no streaks of white are visible. Pour mousse into a pretty bowl or individual serving dishes and refrigerate until set, at least four hours. Just before serving, beat cream in small, chilled mixing bowl until soft peaks form. Garnish mousse with whipped cream and chocolate curls.

Serves 6

Spain: *Flan*
Caramel Custard

½ cup sugar
2 tablespoons water
2 cups milk
2 cups light cream
8 eggs
pinch salt

¾ cup sugar
1½ teaspoon vanilla

To caramelize mold: in a small, heavy saucepan combine sugar and water. Cook over moderate heat, stirring constantly, until sugar melts and turns a golden brown. Quickly pour the syrup into a warmed 6-cup mold (or six custard cups). Stand in hot water. Turn mold or custard cups in all directions so syrup coats both bottom and sides. Set aside.

In a large saucepan, combine milk and cream; scald. Do not let mixture come to a boil. Remove from heat and cool slightly. Preheat oven to 350 degrees.

Meanwhile, in a mixer bowl beat eggs and salt slightly. Add sugar gradually as you continue beating. Add milk and cream slowly, beating constantly; then add vanilla. Pour custard into mold. Place mold in a larger pan filled with hot water that reaches halfway up the sides of the bowl. Bake about one hour or until knife inserted in the center comes out clean. Cool custard in the mold. Place a serving dish on top of mold and invert. Custard should slide out.

Serves 6 to 8

8

Hospitality
and MINISTRY

For as the body apart from the spirit is dead, so also faith apart
from works is dead.

—JAMES 2:26

*A*s I sat down at the computer on a warm Saturday
afternoon, I paused to thank my heavenly Father for
the task I was about to undertake. Bowing my head,
I rehearsed the events of the week—it was quite an exciting
one for my coauthor Lisa and me. Monday we FedEx-ed
Designing a Lifestyle That Pleases God, the companion volume
to *Becoming a Woman Who Pleases God*, to our publisher;
again our Lord graciously multiplied our time, and we were
able to submit it ahead of the contract deadline. However,
to stay within the word limit suggested by the publisher, we
felt we had to eliminate some of the hospitality content. Lisa

had prepared and participated in the first radio interview for *Becoming a Woman Who Pleases God* on Friday, and I was immersed in preparation for the one-hour interview we would share the following week.

Sandwiched in between those activities and the normal living cycle of housecleaning, laundry, grocery shopping, and all of the other tasks necessary to live life, we met on Tuesday to discuss the potential of a third book while Lisa's young sons slept. The aroma of freshly brewed coffee greeted me as she opened the door; the house was cool, the dining room table ready for our work time, and a plate of tasty home-made lemon bars was handy to maintain our nutrition level. Lisa's tender prayer preceded the sharing of our individual resources, and by the time her young sons awoke from their naps we had a working title and the outline of a third book, complete with individual writing assignments.

Hospitality and Practice

"Do you want to be shown, you foolish person, that faith apart from works is useless?" (James 2:20). Lisa and I recorded in *Becoming a Woman Who Pleases God* and *Designing a Lifestyle That Pleases God* a portion of the home economics education that our alumnae from Christian Heritage College and The Master's College received. As we talked about what our new book might contain, we thought that it would add a special dimension if we asked those who have practiced the home economics principles and skills in their own homes to share their ideas with our readers. Thus, my reason for being at the computer on Saturday: to craft a survey that would allow us to draw upon the experiences of our home economics alumnae. At the conclusion of my preparation, I was filled with anticipation as I considered the wealth of information the survey would provide—especially the significant impact its results could have on the body of Christ. As the afternoon drew to a close, I had captured the content that Lisa and I needed in these questions:

- Describe your season of life. For example, I would say, "I am currently a mature, single professional." Dr. Tatlock would say, "I have been married for sixteen years and have five children."
- How do you define hospitality?
- What traditions do you practice in your home that support your lifestyle and marital status?
- How have you used your hospitality skills in ministry?
- If you work with individuals of a different culture, how do you blend their hospitality traditions with yours?
- Identify differences between American cultural traditions and the cultural traditions of the people you are working among.
- How have you used your home as a center for evangelism? How do you share Christ with others in your home?
- What special hospitality tips or recipes would you suggest for our readers?

The response to the survey request was a special blessing; the life experiences that our alumnae shared reflected the various ways that biblical hospitality is practiced.

Tips for Practicing Biblical Hospitality

"And let us not grow weary of doing good, for in due season we will reap, if we do not give up" (Gal. 6:9). We have already enjoyed many of our survey responses, as you saw, reading through the previous chapters. The respondents range in age from recent college graduate to early twenties to mid-forties and married for twenty-three years with four children.[1] We now have the opportunity to gain from the experience of these wise women who represent a variety of seasons of life and reside in a myriad of cultural surroundings.

Ann Banta believes that it is all right not to have everything perfect when her guests arrive, a thought repeated by Lynn Cathy, Lisa DiGiacomo, and Holly Morales. In fact if the guests can help with the finishing touches, they will feel more at ease. It is easier to chat when we are working instead of just staring at one another.

According to Melitsa Barnes, hospitality does not have to be a grand affair; rather, we must be continually looking for the little ways in life to serve and minister to others. Bonnie Bishop reinforces Melitsa's thoughts by adding that not every event has to be an elaborate one. It's okay to keep it simple.

Lynn Cathy suggests that we plan ahead and develop a schedule. Investing in a Crock-Pot and using it is a hospitality approach suggested by Lisa-Ann Chun. She believes it is a great time-saving way to be ready for whatever entertainment opportunities may arise (even for the busy, working woman). Using a Crock-Pot is a wonderful way to have a meal ready when we return home from church on Sunday, and it provides an incentive to invite guests to come home with us for fellowship.

Robin Contreras suggests that we identify what is biblical and what is special about our hospitality style or unique about our traditions, and, while enjoying our personal preferences, that we refrain from a legalistic attitude that expects others to do the same and considers others sinful when they don't practice hospitality the way we do.

Lisa DiGiacomo believes that the most hospitable person is someone who can be herself and not "put on." She encourages us to relax so that others will be able to relax. If someone comes over unannounced and everything isn't as clean as we might have liked, we can graciously receive our guest and offer something to drink. If we are relaxed, others who might come with a burden or need for friendship will feel freer to share their burdens with us. Usually people who stop by unannounced don't care what our house looks like anyway. They are coming to be with us regardless of the state of our home.

Lisa adds that our greatest desire should be to point people to Christ, who is the perfect One; the rest of us are in this life doing the best we can by God's grace to live a life that glorifies him. When we are weak, he is strong. He lived perfectly for us. We should be living a life of gratitude for what he has done for us. This also applies when the meal doesn't turn out perfectly or when our children are not behaving. So if someone catches us unprepared, we can delight in knowing that we aren't perfect and that all we need is Christ's perfection. Christians who lay hold of the fact that they possess Christ's perfection can be free to be themselves around others.

Becky Ellsworth encourages us to plan and work ahead. She recommends preparing a relaxed menu so that we don't have to experience stress and can enjoy the people. Vicki Ferretti offers a number of helpful tips beginning with meal management:

- Clean as you go.
- Set a pretty table.
- Consider your guests when planning meals (allergies, food preferences).
- Cultivate a sensitivity to your home's atmosphere:
  - Turn off the TV. It is amazing how much background noise impacts conversation and a sense of peacefulness.
  - Play music quietly.
  - Try to keep a tidy home so that you won't be embarrassed when someone unexpectedly drops by.
  - Light a candle. It provides a warm feeling, especially if you don't have a fireplace or don't want to build a fire.
  - Decorate according to the seasons.

227

Vicki adds that we should find reasons to practice hospitality and use the good ideas of others. She writes:

My parents and three other couples get together for breakfast every Saturday, rotating houses. I loved the idea, so when I found that there were several women home with babies we started a breakfast group with the purpose of fellowship. We rotate houses, and everyone brings a project to work on (Christmas cards, scrapbooks, crochet work, etc.). Over hot chocolate and bagels we nurse our babies, enjoy our projects, and share stories as well as advice. I have learned a lot about parenting by my friends' modeling it. I can also direct questions I have to moms who are further along than I am. We are from different churches, and we also see hospitality as a potential evangelism tool centered around relationship building.

Vicki suggests using holidays as a reason to invite others to our home:

I have served as hostess for a Christmas open house for church, entertained a class for dessert and games (when I was teaching school), and had an egg coloring during the Easter season. This tradition has advanced to an egg-decorating contest; the competition is stiff, and the preparation starts early with all of us keeping our eyes open for the perfect kit or ideas. Last year Bryan purchased "resurrection eggs" for our niece, and we shared the story of Easter with our family.

Kelli Gleeson recommends that we purpose not to get so caught up in the details of entertaining (how our table setting looks, making sure things turn out perfect, having the *best* food, making sure our home is spotless) because it takes the joy out of being hospitable and appreciating those who enter our home. She adds that most guests are not concerned about those details: "They simply want to spend time with you and your family in your home. You don't want them to sense that you are more worried about the details than just loving and getting to know them. God only wants your service to him. Our goal is to bring glory to him rather than to us."

Erin Hair uses *Quick Cooking* magazines a lot because they have wonderful, easy, and inexpensive recipes. She also keeps ingredients on hand to prepare for unexpected dinner guests and maintains a file of fast dessert recipes.

Anne Johnson suggests keeping your home so that it is not a crisis to have an impromptu visitor. She adds that this is also a ministry to your family or friends. However, do not demand perfection—in decoration or orderliness—before reaching out to others; that is pride, not ministry. She advises, "Trust God to bless others through you and your home, and he will surely bless you in return."

Heather Lanker reminds us that hospitality doesn't have to end in the home. When someone asks for a ride, try to bring along something to eat and drink for the ride, such as a piece of coffee cake. The gesture creates the feeling of being wanted because we took the time to provide an extra touch.

When Debby Lennick reached the portion of the survey that asked for practical tips, she responded:

> This is my favorite part of the survey! A great part of hospitality translates to my home and my cooking. Is my home a place that is prepared and ready for the family and guests? That is my goal. Although I work full time, I want my husband and three daughters to feel free to invite anyone over for dinner or dessert even at the last minute. My goal at any given time is to be able to whip up a meal or dessert to meet the need. We try to keep a well-stocked kitchen to meet most entertaining surprises.

Debby suggests that we teach our children how to work around the house, not only picking up and doing laundry, but also in the area of meal preparation. This is more than just microwaving and turning on a toaster oven. The teaching should include preparing raw and fresh foods from scratch, mixing, baking, stove-top cooking and, yes, the clean-up too. My twenty-year-old daughter cooks dinner one night a week and my sixteen-year-old cooks two or three times a month, while my eight-year-old empties the dishwasher and does other simple age-appropriate tasks. They all help at every meal. This great tool in our home results in a more prepared home. Another outcome of working together is our eating most evening meals as a family. Also, my girls enjoy cooking and providing hospitality to our guests, for which I hope I have been a role model.

Make simple, quick meals with good ingredients. Retain nutritional competency by doing as much of your own preparation as possible; however, using some healthy prepared frozen foods can offer some options. Another good idea is to precook over the weekend. Some of Debby's standard meal scenarios follow.

Cook lean ground beef and/or ground turkey. (I like combining the two meats.) Drain and freeze standard recipe portions flat in resealable plastic bags. Meal ideas for cooked ground meat include adding it to a spaghetti sauce; serving it over rice with soy sauce and a side of green beans; spooning it on tortilla chips for "chip tacos" or super nachos, or combining it with refried beans for burritos; and using it in your favorite casserole.

Simmer chicken breasts (with or without skin and bones) or a beef chuck roast in salted water with a carrot, an onion, and some celery. Discard the cooked vegetables and save the broth. Place the broth in large resealable plastic bags, set upright in a bowl or in plastic freezer containers until solid. Lightly shred the meat and freeze flat in large resealable plastic bags. The same procedure works well with leftover turkey. She suggests the following meal ideas for the chicken and turkey:

- Simmer broth and some chicken with vegetables of choice for soup; add rice or noodles and season to taste.
- Spoon it on tortilla chips for "chip tacos," super nachos, enchiladas, or tacos; or combine it with refried beans for burritos.
- Stir in barbeque sauce for a great sandwich.

- Add to vegetable stir-fry and serve over rice.
- Sauté with a little garlic and onion, and then place on a roll and add cheese.
- Put with lettuce, mayo, mustard, and avocado for a tasty sandwich.
- Season lightly with seasoning salt and pepper and place over rice; top with steamed broccoli and a little soy sauce.
- Use it to enhance a salad.
- Add it to gravy or cream of mushroom soup and serve over mashed potatoes. (Homemade gravy: whisk 1 cup cold broth with 2 tablespoons flour. Bring to a boil and simmer 1–2 minutes. Season to taste. A can of cream of mushroom soup may be used, thinning to desired thickness with water or milk. The color can be darkened by using a few drops of Kitchen Bouquet.)

Debby suggests learning to prepare speedy meals, starting with these suggestions:

Quick, Easy Chicken Dinners

- *Baked chicken*: Lightly season with seasoning salt one breast per person; bake at 350 degrees for one hour. Add an average-size baking potato per person since both require the same cooking time. Serve with vegetables and salad (salad ideas follow).
- *Chicken Parmesan*: Brush one chicken breast per person with olive oil, a teaspoon of prepared crushed garlic (using garlic from a jar is acceptable), and a light sprinkling of Italian seasoning. Bake 50 to 60 minutes at 350 degrees or until tender. Drain liquid and top with your favorite spaghetti sauce. Bake till sauce is hot; add shredded mozzarella and Parmesan cheese and continue baking until cheese is melted. Serve with pasta and a salad.

Do you have a rice cooker? You'll like this one from Debby: for dinner for four, place one and a half cups of uncooked white rice and three cups of water into the rice cooker. (Check package for brand instructions.) Place six frozen, precooked teriyaki chicken breasts atop the uncooked rice. Turn on the rice cooker; in 20 to 25 minutes it's done. Serve with vegetables and salad. (Various other flavored precooked chickens are great too, such as honey-mustard.)

Debby has some good salad ideas, too: add chicken, sliced ham, and some of your favorite shredded or diced cheese to assorted greens. Increase texture by including grapes, mandarin oranges, and either soft or crunchy noodles. When packing a salad to go, make it upside down: put in the salad dressing first, then vegetables, and the lettuce last. Dump it out onto a plate for an impressive salad.

She stresses the importance of knowing your basic flavor-enhancing seasonings, which can be used on beef, chicken, rice, potatoes, and any number of vegetables. Garlic is a great standard. The easiest forms to use are powder or crushed (fresh or purchased in a jar). Using Italian seasoning blend is an easy way to create an Italian flavor; fennel seed is a fabulous addition to an Italian sauce or dish; taco seasoning (cumin is the main ingredient) produces a Mexican taste in meats and rice; ginger produces an Asian zest; curry provides Indian or Moroccan enhancement; and kosher salt is a wonderful salt because it packs more punch than regular salt (use it sparingly).

Dessert? According to Debby, it's easy! Always have on hand vanilla ice cream and chocolate chips. Make a fabulous chocolate sauce in the microwave by mixing ¾ cup of chocolate chips and 1 tablespoon of vegetable oil. Microwave on high for 1 minute. Stir vigorously. Microwave for another 30 seconds. Stir till smooth. Drizzle over ice cream for a fabulous "chocolate shell" effect. Options: top with light whipped cream, peanuts, and strawberries.

Finally, Debby says, maintain good relationships with family members. We always want our husband to be willing to grill for a barbeque dinner and one of our older children to make part of dinner or bake brownies. In a nutshell, moms should not necessarily be doing a solo when it comes to meal prep.

Erin McLeod reminds us to pray for God to help us prepare our heart, not just our home, when we invite others over. It is too easy to be consumed with preparations!

Holly Morales often hears people say not to worry about how our house looks when people visit, but she suggests that our home needs to represent the Lord's orderliness as often as possible. Patti Morse offers a number of tried and true hospitality tips:

- We are not entertaining; we are sharing the love of Christ with others and are ministering to their needs with the intent of blessing their lives.
- Though a beautiful table and well-prepared food are nice, they are not to be the focal point of any gathering. Jesus Christ should always be the focus of our fellowship with others.
- To cut down on stress, prepare as much in advance as we can. Do any chopping or other food preparation and set the table the day before. This leaves time for us to prepare ourselves spiritually and to minister to our guests in tangible ways.
- Do not expect everything to be perfect! Remember, perfection is not the goal of the evening.
- Maintain our sense of humor and be creative if something does not turn out exactly as we had planned. Keep our mind set on things above, not on things below, and our perspective will remain God-honoring.
- Consistently greet our guests with a genuine smile and communicate to them that we feel so blessed to have them in our home. They have honored us by graciously accepting our invitation; perhaps we can greet them outside, and walk them to their car when it is time for them to leave.

- Always begin a meal with prayer, thanking God for our guests. We might have a time of prayer with them before they leave, asking them specifically how we can pray for them. This sensitivity deepens relationships and opens doors for ministry opportunities.
- Fresh flowers, soft music, and candles (at night) are always a nice touch.
- We can fold our napkins so there is a nice little pocket created where we can place a special mint or flower and a Scripture verse for each guest. It doesn't take a lot to make things special—just a little imagination using things already in our home and garden to spruce up a table or setting.
- Conversation "ice breakers" are always fun. Often we will open the dinner conversation with a question for each person to answer, especially if we are not well acquainted with one another. This spontaneity puts people at ease, prompts conversation, and helps us to get to know one another. We might ask, "What is your favorite dessert and why?" or "How did you meet your spouse?"

Connie Naresh encourages us to use the suggestions in this book when preparing for dinners and social events—they really work! She also suggests praying before our guests arrive, asking that God will give us wisdom with each interaction and use us to meet the needs of our guests. She adds that we shouldn't be afraid to try new recipes or methods of preparation for family meals, discussing with our husband how he wants to show hospitality to others and then working hard to facilitate his ideas.

Connie suggests cooking through a cookbook. She finds it helpful to pick a cookbook or two for a season of the year. She plans weekly menus from recipes listed in a particular cookbook and then switches to a new cookbook after she has tried the recipes that fit into her family's diet and preferences. This is also a great way to come up with new dinner ideas to serve to friends and families.

Tracie Priske recommends that we shouldn't feel like we always have to serve a five-course meal. Popcorn and hot chocolate are fun to serve to guests on a chilly evening.

Matt and Amy Raper enjoy inviting new friends over for game nights because it is a fun way to get to know one other, and the atmosphere is usually really relaxed. They find that people warm up quickly, and the evening often ends by planning another game night.

Jalin Rice writes that people enjoy coming over to dinner because they like being invited into our space. She adds an admonition not to worry about the monetary value of our home—just plan, prepare, and invite. Our guests will love being blessed by seeing a family acting like a family—eating and interacting together—especially those who do not have a family model.

Getting together with people with whom we might not normally hang out is Angi Roe's suggestion. She reminds us that it is fun to get to know and learn about new people.

Janell Pantoja recommends that we keep a sense of humor and forget about our pride, because it will be the time we spend that our guest will remember more than the food. She also encourages us to make time to have people over by setting a goal to have guests in our home on a regular basis; but, she adds, this goal should accommodate our lifestyle. She encourages us to pray that God will bring to us people in our church, neighborhood, or work who need someone to talk with. And remember, she adds, we have to be willing to give without getting anything in return.

Peggy Rowan offers some timely dos and don'ts:

- Do put up with little irritations.
- Do put our guest(s) first.
- Do put all our cares and service in the Lord's hands.
- Don't put on airs.

Tammi Schmorleitz suggests themed game nights. Ask guests to participate by bringing food like Mexican nachos, baked potatoes and toppings, salad, or sundae fixings.

Laurie Twibell learned from her husband that those in industry have to define their customers and their needs. She believes that with hospitality we have to make sure to include our own family and not just our guests as our "customers." To implement her philosophy she makes a special effort to do things for her family at mealtime. She then adds a sobering illustration: "I was making a special loaf of bread for a party, and my husband asked, 'Why don't you make that for us?' That was all I needed to hear!"

Maria VanderJagt suggests having an open door policy for our home. Never turn anyone away who needs a place to stay, or food, or a listening ear. Be thankful, she adds, that God has given us a home that we can use to his glory, and remember that our home, car, money, time, are on loan from God and are to be used for his glory and benefit, not ours.

Debby Zacharoff concludes with a reminder to plan social activities with the goal of sharing Christ with our guests—and don't give up doing good (Gal. 6:9).

A Concluding Consideration

Matthew 5:1–12 and Luke 6:20–26 are passages of Scripture that are commonly referred to as the Beatitudes. When describing the Beatitudes John MacArthur writes that *blessed* literally means happy, fortunate, and blissful:

> It speaks of more than a surface emotion. Jesus was describing the divinely bestowed well-being that belongs only to the faithful. The Beatitudes demonstrate that the way to heavenly blessedness is antithetical to the worldly path normally followed in pursuit of happiness. The worldly idea is that happiness is found in riches, merriment, abundance, leisure, and such things. The real truth is the very opposite. The Beatitudes give Jesus' description of the character of true faith.[2]

As *Practicing Hospitality* draws to a close, I want to share with you a word I coined to summarize its contents—*hospitalitude*; it is drawn from the word *hospitality* meaning to pursue the love of strangers and the word *beatitude*—signifying the character of true faith. It is my prayer that *Practicing Hospitality* stimulates you to practice biblical hospitality so that the *Hospitalitudes* will be evident in your life.

Hospitalitudes

- Happy are those who practice biblical hospitality because in so doing they are demonstrating their love for God (1 John 3:17–18).
- Happy are those who pursue the love of strangers for they are choosing to obey their heavenly Father's command and modeling his character (Rom. 12:13b).
- Happy are those in church leadership who practice hospitality for they allow others to observe them in their homes where their character is most graphically revealed (1 Tim. 3:1–2; Titus 1:5–8).
- Happy are those who include people of all cultures on their guest lists for in this manner they are demonstrating the expansive love of their heavenly Father (John 3:16).
- Happy are those who are willing to make the sacrifice to practice hospitality, for they understand that memories require time and energy to create (Ex. 12:1–14).
- Happy are those who develop hospitality management skills, for in this way they are capable of being faithful stewards of all that the Lord has provided for them (1 Cor. 4:2).
- Happy are those who intentionally extend hospitality to "the others"—singles, widows, the grieving, the hospitalized, those with dietary challenges, and those

experiencing food insecurity—for they are choosing to live out biblical compassion (James 2:14–16).

- Happy are those whose homes are both a place of refuge and a center for evangelism for they are glorifying their heavenly Father by their actions (1 Pet. 2:11–12) and fulfilling his instructions to "do the work of an evangelist" (2 Tim. 4:5).

- Happy are those who have consecrated their lives to their heavenly Father, for they are then capable of practicing true biblical hospitality (2 Cor. 4:7).

- Happy are those who have consecrated their china to their Lord's service for they have the opportunity of helping others to "taste and see that the LORD is good" (Ps. 34:8).

- Happy are those who do not become disillusioned in practicing biblical hospitality for they understand that in due time they will reap if they do not grow weary (Gal. 6:9).

- Happy are those who acknowledge that they are unable to practice biblical hospitality in their own strength, for by this means they learn that the Lord's power overcomes their weaknesses and allows them to become vessels used for his honor and glory (2 Cor. 12:9-10; Phil. 4:13).

Practicing Hospitality

1. How do you define hospitality? Support your definition with Scripture.

2. Describe your season of life and the unique opportunities it offers for you to extend biblical hospitality.

3. Evaluate your current involvement in biblical hospitality by responding to the following questions:

- What traditions do you practice in your home that support your lifestyle and marital status?
- How do you use your hospitality skills in ministry?
- If you have opportunities to entertain individuals of a different culture, how can you blend their hospitality traditions with yours?
- How can you expand your borders if you currently do not entertain individuals of a different culture?
- How have you used your home as a center for evangelism (how do you share Christ with others in your home)?
- What goals will you set to love friends and strangers more faithfully?

4. Write each of the Hospitalitudes on a card; meditate on them each time you work in your kitchen.

5. Create your own list of hospitalitudes.

Recipe Resources

Use the "Tips for Cooking for a Crowd" and the "Recipe Adjustment Chart" (see below) to prepare food for large groups.

Tips for Cooking for a Crowd

At times you may be called upon to produce meals for large parties, which will undoubtedly mean adjusting your favorite recipes to accommodate the number of guests. Some tips to make your quantity cooking experience a delight rather than a disaster include remembering that recipe enlargement should be *no more* than four times the original recipe; food scientists recommend two times—if you overexpand you may end up with a number of challenges.

- Choose only those recipes you can prepare with confidence. Practice by converting some of your favorite recipes to a quantity proportion using the Recipe Adjustment Chart that follows and then prepare them. Note the additional preparation and cooking time required to produce the recipe in quantity. I have provided a sample recipe conversion for you.
- Assess your cooking and serving vessels as well as your oven or refrigerator space. Also, prepare the food in several moderate-sized batches. Understand that a longer preparation time is usually needed; this is true for everything from shopping to baking or heating the food.
- Use both the top of your range and the oven if the meal is hot. Limited heating space can be supplemented with small appliances such as an electric skillet (be sure to check your electrical capabilities to avoid losing power by blowing out circuits). Choose foods that are simple enough to prepare so that you have time to add the finishing garnishes that are often characteristic of intimate dinners. Finally, recall that presentation enhances the taste of the meal.

Recipe Adjustment Chart

Standard Recipe for _____

Insert recipe name

Use the Table of Equivalents and Abbreviations to convert standard recipes to quantity recipes.

Ingredient	Standard Recipe Serves ____	2 Times Standard Recipe Serves ___	4 Times Standard Recipe Serves ___

Ingredient	Standard Recipe Serves ____	2 Times Standard Recipe Serves ___	4 Times Standard Recipe Serves ___

Preparation and Cooking Time

Preparation Time for Standard Recipe	Preparation Time for 2 Times Standard Recipe	Preparation Time for 4 Times Standard Recipe
Cooking Time for Standard Recipe	Cooking Time for 2 Times Standard Recipe	Cooking Time for 4 Times Standard Recipe

Recipe Adjustment Chart

Quantity Recipe for Old-fashioned Macaroni and Cheese

Ingredient	Standard Recipe Serves 6	2 Times Quantity Recipe Serves 12	4 Times Quantity Recipe Serves 24
uncooked elbow macaroni (about 2 cups)	6–7 ounces (about 2 cups)	12–14 ounces (about 4 cups)	24–28 ounces (about 8 cups)
grated onion	2 tablespoons	¼ cup	½ cup
shredded sharp cheese	3 cups	6 cups	12 cups
butter	2 tablespoons	¼ cup	½ cup
flour	2 tablespoons	¼ cup	½ cup
salt	½ teaspoon	1 teaspoon	1½ teaspoons
milk	2 cups	4 cups	8 cups

Preparation and Cooking Time

Preparation Time for Standard Recipe	Preparation time for 2 Times Quantity Recipe	Preparation Time for 4 Times Quantity Recipe
1 hour	*1½ hours*	*2 hours*
Cooking Time for Standard Recipe	Cooking Time for 2 Times Quantity Recipe	Cooking Time For 4 Times Quantity Recipe
30 minutes covered *15 minutes uncovered*	*45 minutes covered* *20 minutes uncovered*	*1 hour covered* *30 minutes uncovered*

Table of Equivalents

Measurement	Equals	Equivalent
A few grains	=	Less than ⅛ teaspoon
60 drops	=	1 teaspoon
1 teaspoon	=	⅓ tablespoon
2 tablespoons	=	1 fluid ounce
4 tablespoons	=	¼ cup or 2 ounces
5⅓ tablespoons	=	⅓ cup or 2⅔ ounces
8 tablespoons	=	½ cup or 4 ounces
16 tablespoons	=	1 cup or 8 ounces
¼ cup	=	4 tablespoons
⅜ cups	=	¼ cup + 2 tablespoons
⅝ cup	=	½ cup + 2 tablespoons
⅞ cup	=	¾ cup + 2 tablespoons
1 cup	=	½ pint or 8 fluid ounces
2 cups	=	1 pint or 16 fluid ounces
1 pint liquid	=	16 fluid ounces
1 quart liquid	=	2 pints or 4 cups
1 gallon liquid	=	4 quarts or 16 cups

Abbreviations

f. d.	few drops	oz	ounce
f. g.	few grains	lb	pound
fl oz	fluid ounces	pk	peck
t	teaspoon	bu	bushel
T	tablespoon	mL	milliliter
c	cup	L	liter
pt	pint	g	gram
qt	quart	kg	kilogram
gal	gallon		

List of Contributors

Ann Banta. Married eighteen years with three children; works part time.

Melitsa Barnes. Married two years.

Bonnie Bishop. Single professional.

Lynn Cathy. Married twenty-five years; two teenagers; preschool director.

Lisa-Ann Chun. Newly married; working wife; no children.

Robin Contreras. Married five years; three children.

Lisa DiGiacomo. Married seven years; three daughters.

Sue Edwards. Married twenty-five years; four children.

Becky Ellsworth. Married to a pastor sixteen years; four children.

Vicki Ferretti. Married nine years; three children.

Elizabeth Gilbert. Married nineteen years; thirteen children.

Kelli Gleeson. Married five years; two children.

Anne Goad. Married nineteen years; two children.

Erin Hair. Single professional.

Anne Johnson. Newly married; lives in an apartment; home economics teacher.

Cherie Land. Married nineteen years; two children.

Heather Lanker. Married eight years; two daughters.

Debby Lennick. Married; three daughters; married to her current husband for twelve years; previously a single mom for five years preceded by a ten-year marriage to the father of her two oldest daughters.

Erin McLeod. Married; two children.

Holly Morales. Married twelve years; three children.

Patti Morse. Married twenty-six years; two adult children.

Connie Naresh. Married seven years; two children.

Holly Nyquist. Married; two children; missionary to Bolivia.

Janell Pantoja. Recently married.

Tracie Priske. Married ten years; two children.

Amy Raper. Married five years; one daughter, two sons.

Jalin Rice. Married seven years; three children.

Angi Roe. Married eleven years; two children.

Peggy Rowan. Married twenty-one years; two teenaged sons.

Tammi Schmorleitz. Married twenty years; three children.

Laurie Twibell. Married fourteen years; two children.

Maria VanderJagt. Married five years.

Sandy White. Married twenty-five years; three children; missionary to Turkey.

Deborah Zacharoff. Married twenty-two years; no children; teacher.

Scripture Grids

The scriptural principles upon which chapters of this book were built are given in the eight Scripture Grids on this and the next several pages.

CHAPTER 1

Hospitality and Character
Romans 5:3–4

Theme	Reference
Character—What Is It?	Romans 8:29a
H—humble	1 Peter 5:5b
O—obedient	1 Samuel 15:22b
S—sincere	2 Corinthians 1:12
P—prayerful	1 Thessalonians 5:17
I—integrity	Psalm 25:21
T—trustworthy	Proverbs 31:11
A—adopted	Romans 8:15
L—led by the Spirit	Romans 8:14
I—instrument of righteousness	Romans 6:13
T—thankful	Colossians 3:15
Y—yielded	Romans 6:19

CHAPTER 2

Hospitality and Strangers
Hebrews 13:2

Theme	Reference

Defining Biblical Hospitality
  Motivated by God's love
  Enthusiastically pursue hospitality
	Romans 12:13

Hospitality Lovingly Meets Needs
  Who are the strangers?
  How do you meet needs?
  Hospitality reveals character
	Proverbs 14:31

Hospitality and the Old Testament Hospitality defined	Proverbs 19:17

CHAPTER 3

Hospitality and Family
Proverbs 31:28–31

Theme	Reference
Family First	Proverbs 31:27
Practicing Hospitality with a Family Seven principles	Proverbs 19:14

Family Traditions
  The importance of family traditions
  The interpretation of family traditions
    A spiritual heritage
    A kindred heritage
    A holiday heritage
  The influence of family traditions
	Ecclesiastes 12:1

CHAPTER 4

Hospitality and Management
Colossians 3:23

Theme	Reference
The Importance of Managing	Proverbs 14:23
Refuse Idleness	Proverbs 31:27
Manage Your Home	Titus 2:3–5
Prepare for Graciousness	Proverbs 11:16a

CHAPTER 5

Hospitality and Your Home
1 Peter 2:11–12

Theme	Reference
The Home as a Place of Refuge	Psalm 91:1–2
The Home as a Center for Evangelism	1 Timothy 6:18
Consecrating Our China for Our Master's Use	Numbers 7:10–13

Hostessing a Consecrated China Tea
• Teatime tidbits
• Teatime testimonies
• The anatomy of an outreach tea—practical
  examples from missionaries serving in
  Bolivia and Turkey
	Psalm 34:8

CHAPTER 6

Hospitality and Others
James 2:14–16

Theme	Reference
Biblical Compassion—What Is It?	Mark 8:1–2

Hospitality as a Way of Displaying Compassion
• Singles (as an invited guest and the initiator
  of guests)
• Widows (as an invited guest and the initiator
  of guests)
• The grieving
• The hospitalized (the family and the patient)
• Guests with dietary challenges
• Individuals experiencing food insecurity (low-
  income, poverty, the homeless)
• The elderly
• Compassion and food security
	Matthew 25:40

CHAPTER 7

Hospitality and Culture
1 Corinthians 9:19, 23

Theme	Reference
Culture Impacts Hospitality	1 Corinthians 9:22
What Is Culture?	1 Corinthians 10:31–33

Culture and Hospitality
    Time orientation
    Task/Goal focus
    Etiquette
Food
	Proverbs 31:20

Internationals in Our Backyard	Acts 10:34–35

CHAPTER 8

Hospitality and Ministry
James 2:26

Theme	Reference
Hospitality and Practice	James 2:20
Tips for Practicing Hospitality	Galatians 6:9

Recipe Index

Recipe Index

Recipe Index

Notes

Introduction

1. See chapter 8 for a description and questions.

Chapter 1: Hospitality and Character

1. http://www.charactercounts.org.
2. Ibid.
3. See John MacArthur, *Think Biblically! Recovering a Christian Worldview* (Wheaton, IL: Crossway Books, 2003), 169–86, for elaboration.
4. John MacArthur, *The MacArthur Study Bible* (Nashville, TN: Word, 1997), note at Matthew 5:3.
5. John MacArthur, *The MacArthur Study Bible*, notes at John 14:15 and John 14:21–24.
6. See Pat Ennis and Lisa Tatlock, *Designing a Lifestyle That Pleases God* (Chicago: Moody, 2004), 45.
7. John MacArthur, *The MacArthur Study Bible*, notes at Romans 12:9–21.
8. See "List of Contributors" in this volume.
9. Donna Morley, *Choices That Lead to Godliness* (Wheaton, IL: Crossway Books, 1999), 169.
10. John MacArthur, *The MacArthur Study Bible*, notes at Philippians 1:10.
11. John MacArthur, *Lord Teach Me to Pray* (Nashville, TN: J. Countryman, 2003), 19.
12. *Random House Webster's College Dictionary*, 2nd ed., s.v. "integrity."
13. Ibid., s.v. "integer."
14. John MacArthur, *The MacArthur Study Bible*, notes at Philippians 1:10.
15. Robert Munger, *My Heart, Christ's Home* (Downers Grove, IL: InterVarsity, 1954).
16. A helpful resource for *trustworthy* is Nancy Leigh DeMoss, *Elizabeth: Lessons on Grace and Faith from the Life of an Older Woman*. Visit the Revive Our Hearts web site for ordering information (http://www.LifeAction.org).
17. See Pat Ennis and Lisa Tatlock, *Designing a Lifestyle That Pleases God*, 174.
18. John MacArthur, *The MacArthur Study Bible*, notes at Romans 6:12.
19. John MacArthur, *The MacArthur Study Bible*, notes at Philippians 4:8.
20. See "List of Contributors."

Notes

21. Russell Cronkhite, *A Return to Sunday Dinner* (Sisters, OR: Multnomah, 2003), 195.
22. *Random House Webster's College Dictionary*, 2nd ed., s.v. "principle."

Chapter 2: Hospitality and Strangers

1. Romans 12:1–2 (NKJV).
2. John MacArthur, *The MacArthur Study Bible* (Nashville, TN: Word, 1997), 1716.
3. Ibid., 34.
4. Steve Wilkins, *Face to Face: Meditations on Friendship and Hospitality* (Moscow, ID: Canon Press, 2002), 90.
5. Survey responses are paraphrases of the original.
6. *Vines Expository Dictionary of Biblical Words*, s.v. "philoxenia."
7. John MacArthur, *The MacArthur Study Bible*, 1717.
8. See the *New International Version Study Bible* (Grand Rapids, MI: Zondervan, 1985), 1876, note on Hebrews 13:2.
9. *Vines Expository Dictionary of Biblical Words*, s.v. "entertain."
10. Alexander Strauch, *The Hospitality Commands* (Littleton, CO: Lewis & Roth, 1993), 43.
11. Fred H. Wight, *Manners and Customs of Bible Lands* (Chicago: Moody, 1953), 69.
12. Merrill F. Unger, *Unger's Bible Dictionary* (Chicago: Moody, 1961), 502.
13. James M. Freeman, *Manners and Customs of the Bible*. (Plainfield, NJ: Logos International, 1972), 16–17.
14. Fred H. Wight, *Manners and Customs of Bible Lands*, 70.
15. Ibid.
16. James M. Freeman, *Manners and Customs of the Bible*, 223.
17. Alexander Strauch, *The Hospitality Commands*, 38.

Chapter 3: Hospitality and Family

1. Dorothy Kelley Patterson, *A Handbook for Ministers' Wives* (Nashville, TN: Broadman & Holman, 2002), 104.
2. Carolyn Mahaney, *Feminine Appeal* (Wheaton, IL: Crossway Books, 2003), 21.
3. See List of Contributors: Peggy Rowan.
4. See List of Contributors: Tammi Schmorleitz.
5. See List of Contributors: Patti Morse.
6. See List of Contributors: Laurie Twibell.
7. For more information on how to manage your home, see chapter 4, "The Wise Woman Manages Her Home," in Pat Ennis and Lisa Tatlock, *Becoming a Woman Who Pleases God: A Guide to Developing Your Biblical Potential* (Chicago: Moody, 2003).
8. *Thorndike and Barnhart Advanced Dictionary*, 2nd ed. (Upper Saddle River, NJ: Scott Foresman: 1974), s.v. "tradition."
9. Ibid., s.v. "heritage."
10. Dorothy Kelley Patterson, *A Handbook for Ministers' Wives*, 108.
11. Noël Piper, *Treasuring God in Our Traditions* (Wheaton, IL: Crossway Books, 2003), 26.
12. J. Otis Ledbetter and Tim Smith, *Family Traditions* (Colorado Springs, CO: Chariot Victor, 1998), 11.
13. Edith Schaeffer, *What Is a Family?* (Grand Rapids, MI: Baker Books, 1975), 183–84.
14. Ibid., 188.
15. Noël Piper, *The Family Treasury of Great Holiday Ideas* (Uhrichsville, OH: Barbour, 1998).

Chapter 4: Hospitality and Management

1. Harry Nobles, *Hotel Online Special Report: The Legend of the Pineapple* (http://www.hotel-online.com).

2. http://www.waterburyregion.com/visit/pineapple.html.

3. Ibid.

4. Ibid.

5. *Thorndike Barnhart Advanced Dictionary*, 2nd ed. (Upper Saddle River, NJ: Scott Foresman: 1974), s.v. "manage." Definition based on the synonym study of "manage," "conduct," and "direct," 624.

6. Ibid., s.v. "organize."

7. Ibid., s.v. "plan."

8. See "The Wise Woman Manages Her Home," in Patricia Ennis and Lisa Tatlock, *Becoming a Woman Who Pleases God* (Chicago: Moody, 2003).

9. Steve Wilkins, *Face to Face: Meditations on Friendship and Hospitality* (Moscow, ID: Canon Press, 2002), 134.

10. *Thorndike Barnhart Advanced Dictionary*, s.v. "idle."

11. For more information on how to manage your home with excellence see "The Wise Woman Manages Her Home," in Pat Ennis and Lisa Tatlock, *Becoming a Woman Who Pleases God*.

12. John MacArthur, *Different by Design* (Wheaton, IL: Victor, 1994), 70–71.

13. I. D. E. Thomas, *The Golden Treasury of Puritan Quotations*, "Idleness" (Carlisle, PA: Banner of Truth, 2000), 154.

14. Steve Wilkins, *Face to Face: Meditations on Friendship and Hospitality* (Moscow, ID: Canon Press, 2002), 139.

15. For more information on how to clean or establish a cleaning schedule, see "A Wise Woman Manages Her Home with Excellence," in Pat Ennis and Lisa Tatlock, *Becoming a Woman Who Pleases God*.

16. Joann Cairns, *Welcome Stranger, Welcome Friend* (Springfield, MO: Gospel, 1988), 96.

17. *Thorndike Barnhart Advanced Dictionary*, s.v. "gracious."

18. For more information on meal management and hospitality, see "The Wise Woman Practices Biblical Hospitality," in Patricia Ennis and Lisa Tatlock, *Becoming a Woman Who Pleases God*.

19. The original concept of a *hospitality notebook* is taken from Yvonne G. Baker, *The Art of Hospitality* (Denver, CO: Accent, 1986), 13–15. Ideas for various sections in the notebook have been changed and/or modified.

20. Doris W. Greig, *We Didn't Know They Were Strangers* (Ventura, CA: Regal, 1987), 1.

Chapter 5: Hospitality and Your Home

1. *Random House Webster's College Dictionary*, 2nd ed. (New York: Random House, 1997), s.v. "refuge."

2. See Pat Ennis and Lisa Tatlock, "The Wise Woman Develops a Heart of Contentment," in *Becoming a Woman Who Pleases God: A Guide to Developing Your Biblical Potential* (Chicago: Moody, 2003).

3. See "List of Contributors" in this volume.

4. See "List of Contributors."

5. Michael Green, *Evangelism in the Early Church* (Grand Rapids, MI: Eerdmans, 1970), 236.

6. Ibid., 207.

7. Vonette Bright and Barbara Ball, *The Joy of Hospitality* (Orlando, FL: Lifeway, 1996), 32.

8. John MacArthur, *The MacArthur Study Bible* (Nashville, TN: Word, 2000), notes at 2 Timothy 4:5.

9. See "List of Contributors."

10. *Random House Webster's College Dictionary*, s.v. "consecrate."

11. Frances Havergal, *Kept for the Master's Use* (Chicago: Moody, 1999), 23.

12. Emilie Barnes, *If Teacups Could Talk* (Eugene, OR: Harvest House, 1994), 9.

13. Ibid.

Notes

14. A number of tea resources are available including Emilie Barnes, *An Invitation to Tea: Special Celebrations with Treasured Friends* (Eugene, OR: Harvest House, 1996); Emilie Barnes, *If Teacups Could Talk;* Emilie Barnes and Anne Christian Buchanan, *Join Me for Tea* (Eugene, OR: Harvest House, 2002); Emilie Barnes, *Let's Have a Tea Party* (Eugene, OR: Harvest House, 1997); Emilie Barnes, *The Twelve Teas of Celebration: Festive Teas for Special Moments* (Eugene, OR: Harvest House, 2003); Emilie Barnes, *The Twelve Teas of Christmas: Sharing the Season with Those You Love* (Eugene, OR: Harvest House, 1999); Emilie Barnes and Anne Christian Buchanan, *Welcome Home* (Eugene, OR: Harvest House, 1997); Tricia Foley and Catherine Calvert, *Having Tea: Recipes & Table Settings* (New York: Clarkson Potter, 1987); Linda Fraser, *The Perfect Afternoon Tea Book* (New York: Lorenz, 2000); Gail Greco, *Tea-Time at the Inn: A Country Inn Cookbook* (Nashville, TN: Rutledge Hill Press, 1991); Dawn Hylton Gottlieb and Diane Sedo, *Taking Tea with Alice: Looking-Glass Tea Parties and Fanciful Victorian Teas* (New York: Warner Treasures, 1997); Dorothea Johnson, *Tea Etiquette: Taking Tea for Business and Pleasure* (Sterling, VA: Capital,1998); M. Dalton King, *Special Teas* (New York: Smithmark, 1996); Elizabeth Knight, *Tea with Friends* (Pownal, VT: Storey Books,1998); Diana Rosen, *Taking Time for Tea* (North Adams, MA: Storey Books, 2000); Ellyn Sanna, *An Invitation to Tea: A Celebration of Tea & Good Friends* (Uhrichsville, OH: Barbour, 2000); Helene Siegel, Karen Gillingham, *The Totally Teatime Cookbook* (Berkeley, CA: Celestial Arts, 1995); Beulah Munshower Sommer and Pearl Dexter, *Tea with Presidential Families* (Scotland, CT: Olde English Tea Company, 1999); Nan Taylor, *The Graceful Art of Tea* (Santa Clarita, CA: Taylor-Brown, 2003); Mathew Tekulsky, *Making Your Own Gourmet Tea Drinks: Black Teas, Green Teas, Scented Teas, Herb Teas, Iced Teas, and More!* (New York: Crown, 1995).

15. See Pat Ennis and Lisa Tatlock, "The Wise Woman Practices Biblical Hospitality," in *Becoming a Woman Who Pleases God*; and "The Wise Woman Cultivates a Hostess's Heart," in *Designing a Lifestyle That Pleases God* (Chicago: Moody, 2004).

16. See "List of Contributors."

17. Contact Laura Leathers at http://www.teatimetreasures.com for purchasing suggestions.

18. For more information visit her web site at http://www.teatimetreasures.com.

Chapter 6: Hospitality and Others

1. David H. Roper, "The Boxcar Wall," in *Our Daily Bread*, July 30, 2002, Radio Bible Class (Grand Rapids, MI).

2. Jessica Nelson North, *The Pink Book of Verse for Very Little Children* (New York: Sheed & Ward, 1931), 120.

3. http://www.geocities.com/Heartland/2328/wisdom.htm.

4. *Random House Webster's College Dictionary*, 2nd ed. (New York: Random House, 1997), s.v. "hospitality."

5. *Random House Webster's College Dictionary*, s.v. "compassion."

6. Joseph M. Stowell, *Strength for the Journey: Day by Day with Jesus* (Chicago: Moody, 2002), 46.

7. *Random House Webster's College Dictionary*, s.v. "single."

8. http://www.unmarried.org.

9. Nancy Leigh DeMoss, *Singled Out for Him: Embracing the Gift, the Blessings, and the Challenges of Singleness* (Niles: MI: Life Action Ministries, 1998), 15.

10. Ibid., 41–42.

11. *Random House Webster's College Dictionary*, s.v. "widow."

12. http://www.aarp.org/griefandloss/articles/93_a.html.

13. See Pat Ennis and Lisa Tatlock, *Becoming a Woman Who Pleases God: A Guide to Developing Your Biblical Potential* (Chicago: Moody, 2002), 273–78.

14. See "List of Contributors" in this volume.

15. http://www.cdc.gov/nchs/hus.html.

16. See http://www.umassmed.edu/diabeteshandbook/chapo6.htm for exchange charts.

17. http://www.lafightshunger.org/statistics.html.

18. http://www.alpha.scvnet.net/foodpantry.

19. http://www.rmsyr.org/helpus.

20. Gin Phillips, "The Driver behind Meals on Wheels," in *American Profile* (Nashville: Publishing Group of America, 2003), 6–10.

21. Tom Hegg, *A Cup of Christmas Tea* (Minneapolis: Waldman House Press, 1982).

22. Tom Hegg, *A Memory of Christmas Tea* (Minneapolis: Waldman House Press, 1999).

Chapter 7: Hospitality and Culture

1. John MacArthur, *The MacArthur Study Bible* (Nashville, TN: Word, 1997), note on 1 Cor. 9:20, "became as a Jew," 1742.

2. Ibid., note on 1 Cor. 9:22, "weak," 1742.

3. *An American Friend Handbook* (Colorado Springs, CO: International Students, Inc., 1995), 15.

4. Roger E. Axtell, ed., *Do's and Taboos Around the World* (New York: John Wiley & Sons, 1993), 124.

5. Ibid. See gift-giving guidelines for "Austria," 54; "The Czech Republic," 55; and "Germany," 60.

6. Roger E. Axtell, ed., *Do's and Taboos Around the World*, 55.

7. *An American Friend Handbook*, 11.

8. Ibid., 25–26.

9. *Foreign Missions in Your Own Backyard*, (Colorado Springs, CO: International Students, Inc., 1994), 9.

10. Tom Phillips and Bob Norsworthy with Terry Whalin, *The World at Your Door* (Minneapolis: Bethany, 1997), 84.

11. Ibid.

12. Ibid., 85.

13. *Foreign Missions in Your Own Backyard*, 2.

14. *Becoming a Friend with an International Student* (Colorado Springs, CO: International Students, Inc., 1997), 1.

15. You can visit their web site at http://www.ISI.org, or write to them at P.O. Box C, Colorado Springs, CO 80901.

16. Jan Johnson, *Growing Compassionate Kids* (Nashville, TN: Upper Room, 2001), 39.

17. Patrick Johnstone, *Operation World: The Day-by-Day Guide to Praying for the World* (Grand Rapids, MI: Zondervan, 1993).

Chapter 8: Hospitality and Ministry

1. See "List of Contributors" in this volume.

2. John MacArthur, *The MacArthur Study Bible* (Nashville, TN: Word, 2000), notes at Matthew 5:3.